R Brown #

dilithium Press Series on CP/M

How to Get Started with CP/M
Carl Townsend

Practical Guide to CP/M
Carl Townsend

How to Get Started with CP/M®

(Control Program for Microcomputers)

How to Get Started with CP/M®

(Control Program for Microcomputers)

Carl Townsend

dilithium Press
Beaverton, Oregon

NOTE

CP/M, as used in this book, is a registered trade-mark of Digital Research, Inc. of Pacific Grove, California. No other manufacturer can develop an operating system and call it "CP/M." This also protects the user, as any CP/M Operating System you purchase must use the same version of the Digital Research CP/M.

ISBN: 0-918398-32-0
Library of Congress catalog card number: 80-70783

Printed in the United States of America.

dilithium Press
P.O. Box 606
Beaverton, Oregon 97075

Table of Contents

Introduction

"CP/M based micros may be the best supported computers in the world."

Larry Press, President of SSG
in *Intelligent Machine's Journal*

"There is no doubt that the most widely used disk operating system for the microcomputer is CP/M."

Byte Magazine
September 1979

The CP/M Operating System has already become the most widely used operating system for microcomputers. There are more programs, utilities, and suppliers for this operating system than for any system on the market.

Unfortunately, very little of this is documented in a form that can be read and understood by someone unfamiliar with computers. This two-volume user's manual is, hopefully, a step in this direction.

This first volume is a beginner's manual, covering the basics of starting with CP/M. The more complex features are purposely omitted to avoid confusing the beginner. Users should read this book with their standard CP/M documentation handy.

The second volume is written for those who have already been using CP/M, and covers more advanced applications as modems, software, and data base management.

CHAPTER 1

Who Needs an Operating System?

Now that you've purchased your own microcomputer system, you are probably anxious to start using it to do your accounting, word processing, or mailing list. Your powerful hardware system is ready to do your work with any desired program. Your program is on a disk, a tape, or perhaps just on paper. How do you get that program into the computer so you can use it? How do you start the program? How do you copy it, modify it, or print it out? How indeed? You need a program to handle the details of running the hardware and software so you can get on with your application.

THE OPERATING SYSTEM

An **operating system** is a program or, more accurately group of programs, which manages your hardware resources (the computer and peripherals) and software resources (your programs) and interfaces all of these together with you, the user. The operating system calls up the application program you requested and runs it. When your program has finished its job or if it makes an error, control returns to the operating system.

An operating system is a group of programs that organizes a collection of hardware devices and other programs into an integrated system that people can use.

The operating system gives intelligence to the hardware. Some operating systems are very simple, take very little of the computer's memory, and can be found published in magazine articles. Others are very complex, require man-years of effort to develop, and are very sophisticated.

SOFTWARE AND HARDWARE – WHICH IS WHICH?

Computer resources such as the operating system and the computer can be classified as either **hardware** or **software**. Hardware has physical visibility. It can be touched, moved, or consumed. Hardware cannot be protected (generally) by copyrights, trademarks, or patents. In some cases specific mechanical features of machines (as printers) are patented, but with these exceptions the market is open. Hardware includes the computer, memory boards, the disk drives, the printer, ribbons, paper, keyboards, and cables.

Software has no physical visibility. It has value because of its information content. Software can be copyrighted, and generally cannot be copied except for one's own use. As information, it represents intelligence. Application programs, the operating system, user manuals, and program listings are all software.

Some resources are in a gray area that is neither strictly software nor hardware. These include the small program that loads the monitor to the computer when the computer is turned on. This program is stored permanently in the computer in a special circuit. Programs are generally software, but when they are stored on a piece of hardware in this way the issue is complicated. Such resources are called **firmware** to distinguish them from either the software or hardware class.

OPERATING SYSTEM COMPONENTS

An operating system is software, consisting of two primary components:

1. A monitor, also called a supervisor or executive.
2. An integrated set of support utilities.

The relationship of these to each other and to the hardware, user, and application program is shown in Figure 1. Notice that the monitor acts as the interface between the application programs, program utilities and the hardware. The application programs run under control of the monitor and in operation can even use certain parts of the monitor.

THE MONITOR

The **monitor** is an integrated set of programs and routines that forms the interface between the hardware, the user, and the

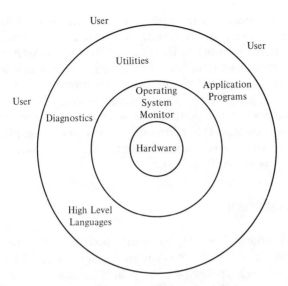

Figure 1. System Overview

application program. The microcomputer monitor has three basic functions:

1. To initialize the system for start-up, setting system parameters as necessary.
2. To initiate and control application program execution.
3. To prioritize and control all input and output operations.

In larger systems the monitor has additional functions such as keeping track of computer time by account numbers, memory management (who gets how much memory and when), and managing processor time between users. With a single user these additional features are generally not needed.

The monitor is normally stored on a disk and loaded immediately when the system is turned on. A very short program, called a **bootstrap loader**, is permanently stored in the computer as firmware to perform the actual loading function. Once the monitor is loaded it waits for a command for the user.

The monitor also initializes the system hardware and peripheral devices. If you add a printer to your system, the monitor portion of the program must be altered to properly initialize the computer circuits that control the printer. This initialization is performed whenever the system is first turned on or reset.

The monitor has two portions: a **kernel** that always remains in the computer memory with your application program and a reloadable **transient** portion. When the monitor is first loaded both parts are loaded to the computer memory. The kernel always remains in memory to moderate system operation. The transient portion is normally over-written by the running application program. This allows more room for the application program. After the program execution is complete, the transient portion is reloaded from disk.

THE UTILITIES

System utilities are portions of the operating system that run under the control of the monitor and perform useful functions at a system level. These functions include file copying, file printing, editing, and debugging. These are functions most people use on a rather continuous and broad-based level, and they are normally provided as a part of the operating system.

There are three types of system utilities:

1. Program development utilities.
2. System management utilities.
3. File management utilities.

Program development utilities include assemblers, editors, interpreters, compilers, linkers, and debuggers. If you are a businessman with a system, you will probably seldom use these unless you plan to develop your own application programs. The one exception might be the editor, as it can serve a variety of functions including limited word processing.

System management utilities are of a very limited nature in microcomputer systems, as there is generally only one user at a time. These include programs to monitor user time against account numbers, diagnostic routines, and system generators to create new operating systems.

File management utilities are the ones most frequently used by the applications-oriented user. These include programs for copying files, erasing files, printing files, renaming files, and checking file status.

PURCHASING AN OPERATING SYSTEM

If you are purchasing an operating system, you should have a list of questions for your salesman. The decision of which operating system to purchase is one of the most important decisions you will make, as it determines to a great extent what you can do with the hardware.

How reliable is the software? Unreliable operating systems can hang up at the wrong time, erase files by mistake, and do other unusual operations. Valuable time can be lost. If the hardware has problems and your application program has a problem, adding an unreliable operating system will add a third variable to your frustration. How long has the operating system been on the market? How many users have it? Are the users happy? Systems that have been on the market several years with thousands of users generally have eliminated all major problems.

How easy is it to modify the operating system? Suppose you wish to add a printer or modem to the system at a later time. Can the system be easily changed without having to call the guy who wrote the operating system? Most operating systems will only work with the hardware of a single manufacturer. This increases the sales of the manufacturer, but does not help you find the most cost-effective hardware system. If you wish to add a printer from another manufacturer, you could discover problems. Even standard RS-232 connections vary considerably in interfacing. Can you get a source listing of the entire I/O control portion of the system? If the salesman hedges on this, beware!

How easy is it to use? Good, easy to read documentation is essential. The system should also catch normal user mistakes to prevent lost files, disk overflow, and such.

How extensive are the utilities? Every utility you have to write or buy will cost you money, and plenty of it. Utilities that come with the system can be sold inexpensively because the development cost is shared by many users. The same operating system may have extra utilities when purchased from certain vendors.

How much does the system cost? The same operating system can have a different price, depending upon the vendor. More money doesn't necessarily mean a better system, but could mean extra features that you might need are included.

How popular is the operating system? A popular system with many users means that many common application programs will already be written and on the market. A new or strange operating system means you may have to write your own accounting program or word processor. If you have some specific application programs you plan to purchase, buy the operating system that will support these programs. Check the quality of the user group for your operating system. A good user group will have plenty of support software.

What special features does the system support? You may need special features for certain applications such as multi-user support or an interrupt-driven operating system. Buy only the features you need, as extra features can be very expensive.

PROTECTION AND COPYRIGHT

Any operating system represents man-years of development effort and therefore represents a large development expense. This development requires specialized skills and requires someone with a knowledge of systems, software, computer architecture, and hardware features. Scarcely a decade ago such development expenses were shared by a relatively small user base and the software costs to purchase any operating system were extremely high. With the advent of the microcomputer systems, the user base for most operating systems has become much larger. This large user base means that microcomputer operating systems can generally be sold at a low cost. Although low in cost, they have high value and are almost always copyrighted. Most systems also have embedded serial numbers or other features to fingerprint the system and make it easy to trace illegal copies back to their source. This copyright protects the author and his investment.

Any copy you have of the operating system must have this copyright notice—manuals, disk, or whatever. The license agreement you receive with the operating system defines your agreement with respect to using the program. Do not loan your operating system to anyone or permit anyone to use it unsupervised, as its control remains your responsibility as the purchaser. The cost of the operating system is low compared with the total hardware system. Don't abuse your product. By protecting the author, you will assure that these gifted authors will continue to enhance their products at a low cost, as well as giving us new products at reasonable prices.

EXERCISES

1. Label each of the following as software, hardware, or firmware:
   a. memory card
   b. connecting cable to disk
   c. a program on a diskette
   d. an empty diskette
   e. the operating system
   f. the operating system user's manual
   g. a bootstrap program on read only memory
   h. printed output on paper
2. Define and give examples of each:
   a. operating system
   b. monitor
   c. hardware
   d. software
3. What are the two components of the system monitor?
4. Distinguish between the monitor and operating system.
5. What are the three functions of the system monitor in a single-user microcomputer system?

CHAPTER 2

CP/M Overview

The CP/M Operating System was written by Digital Research and the letters are an abbreviation for Control Program for Microcomputers. It is by far the most widely accepted operating system for single user microcomputer systems, and some version of it is available for almost every microcomputer system manufactured. A survey of its primary features indicates why this system is so popular.

CP/M is extremely reliable, having been used in the field since 1975. It is widely tested, and the latest version has no known bugs or errors.

CP/M is easy to modify or alter. All I/O operations are controlled from a separate BIOS module, of which the user generally has a source listing. To alter CP/M, it is only necessary to change this source listing, reassemble, and then generate a new system.

Documentation of CP/M is complete. The set of manuals included with CP/M describe the theory and design concepts of the monitor, as well as including user instructions for all utilities.

The cost of CP/M is approximately $150-250, depending upon the target hardware system. This makes it probably one of the lowest cost operating systems on the market. Digital Research (the marketing corporation for CP/M) has maintained this low price to establish a large user base and a high degree of microcomputer system software standardization.

The popularity of CP/M makes it possible to select from a large number of application programs. As a user, you can select from a variety of word processors, accounting programs, and special purpose software. A look at Appendix C will give you a good overview of this support software.

The CP/M system includes a powerful editor, an assembler, and a debugger. The user may purchase from Digital Research or the CP/M user's group such additional support utilities as a macro-assembler, symbolic debugger, a wide variety of high-level languages, and text formatter. The CP/M editor and formatter was used to set-up and edit portions of the manuscript for this book.

HARDWARE REQUIREMENTS FOR CP/M

The minimum hardware requirements for CP/M include:

1. An 8080, Z80 or equivalent central processor.
2. About 20K of memory.
3. A floppy disk drive and controller or hard disk.
4. Some type of keyboard and either a display or printer.

With most systems today the first three items are sold as a single unit. Memory size should also be increased to at least 48,000 bytes of memory to run most popular applications programs.

THE COMPONENTS OF CP/M

The CP/M operating system always loads in the highest part of the computer's memory. For this reason if you ever expand your memory, CP/M must be re-configured before this additional memory can be used. CP/M also uses 256 bytes at the low end of the memory. Each 256 bytes of memory is called a *page*. CP/M uses the first page, and any application programs must be loaded to start at the second page. Most software products take this into consideration, but care must be exercised with systems such as the Radio Shack TRS-80 which use read-only memory. Often CP/M components or application programs must be moved in these systems; special CP/M software suppliers support these systems (see Appendix B).

To a user, CP/M will appear to have two parts. One is a proprietary part that is independent of the system. The other, called the **BIOS**, is a non-proprietary part that is altered by every manufacturer for their own system. The BIOS can, in fact, be altered by the user as peripherals are added or changed.

Technically, CP/M is divided into three components. The proprietary part is considered to be two components. The first is called the **BDOS**, the second the **CCP**. The three components can now be defined as:

BIOS — (Basic Input/Output System). Basic input and output routines. This module is hardware dependent, and a source listing will probably be supplied with your system. It is altered when peripherals are added or changed.

BDOS — (Basic Disk Operating System). Disk manager and software for dynamic file allocation. This is hardware independent.

CCP — (Console Command Processor). Reads and interprets commands from the console. This is hardware independent.

The BIOS always loads in the highest part of the computer's memory, and the rest of CP/M loads below this. The BIOS normally requires 512 bytes of memory or two pages, but if a manufacturer decides to use a longer BIOS, the remaining portion of CP/M can easily be adjusted to this.

Figure 2 shows a memory map of CP/M version 1.4. Notice the BIOS at the very high end of memory and the reserved first page. The BDOS loads below the BIOS and the CCP loads below the BDOS. The BIOS and BDOS together are often referred to as a single module called the **FDOS** (Functional Disk Operating System). The remaining part of the memory not used by CP/M is called the Transient Program Area or **TPA**. Your application programs as well as the CP/M utilities are loaded to the TPA as they are used. While the organization of the segments will be the same for all versions of CP/M, the actual number of bytes in the BIOS segment will vary some from system to system. Consult your system documentation for the size of the BIOS supplied with your system.

Application programs do not use the CCP, and a lengthy program will overlay that area. The FDOS (or the BDOS and the BIOS together) is often used by application programs for disk access (see CP/M Interface Guide), and overlaying into this area can cause problems.

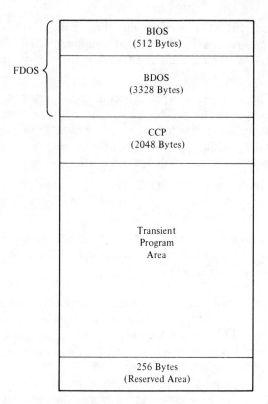

Figure 2. CP/M memory map

VERSIONS OF CP/M

CP/M is now made in a variety of versions for different systems. These can be summarized as:

    1.4 — This is the oldest and most popular version of CP/M on the market with probably over 200,000 users. It is a single user system and will work with 8080, Z80, or 8085 processors.

    2.0 — This is the latest single-user version and has improved disk management routines. It can also be interfaced with hard disks.

    MP/M — This is a real-time multi-tasking operating system which can operate as a multi-user system.

Other versions of CP/M are available for the sixteen bit processors and include additional features.

EXERCISES:

1 . What are the minimum hardware requirements for CP/M?
2. What are the three components of CP/M? Define each
3. Using the criteria of Chapter 1, compare CP/M with one other microcomputer operating system.

CHAPTER 3

Shopping for CP/M Hardware

A wide variety of manufacturers now make hardware that will support CP/M. Although there is a wide variety of hardware, most is generally one of three types:

1. Hardware specifically designed for CP/M using the popular S-100 bus.
2. Hardware specifically designed for CP/M that does not use the S-100 bus.
3. Machines not designed for CP/M but which have been converted to CP/M.

In purchasing hardware, you should be aware of the advantages and disadvantages of each of these categories.

THE S-100 BUS

The S-100 bus-type computer is an early microcomputer design that attracted many users. Many predicted its demise as new, more advanced systems emerged — but the S-100 lives on as a stronger product than ever.

The S-100 computer, now made by many manufacturers, uses a cabinet with a power supply and a heavy-duty interconnect board with from ten (or even fewer) to perhaps twenty sockets. Each socket has a hundred connections, not all of which are used. The heavy-duty board is called the **mother board** and other functional boards, known as **daughter boards**, plug into the sockets on the mother board. Daughter boards can be plugged into any open socket, as their relative position is not important. Normally the processor is on one board, the disk controller on another board, and one or more boards are used for memory. These boards are made by dozens of manufacturers.

Not all of the pins on the connectors are needed, and in the early days of the microcomputer every manufacturer had their own definition of how these pins should work in *their* system. In addition, there were noise problems in reading and writing disks. All of these problems have been solved by the major manufacturers, and the S-100 bus has been standardized to improve compatibility between manufacturers. Beware, however! All S-100 products are still not compatible, and you can still have problems mixing S-100 products, particularly dynamic memories and disk controllers.

The S-100 systems are highly modular. You can expand and update the system as you wish. Modem boards, music synthesizers, computer graphic displays, and voice synthesizers are all available. Hard disk controllers and sixteen bit processors for S-100 systems are already on the market.

There are some disadvantages, however. The larger number of gold-plated connectors and extra boards in these systems mean higher system cost. Also, because of the large number of connectors, reliability may not be as good as in some composite systems. The systems are also generally larger and take more space. Some manufacturers of the better S-100 systems include Systems Group, Delta Products and TEI.

CP/M HARDWARE WITHOUT THE S-100

If you are a businessman you probably won't need music synthesizers or special graphics, but you will want the flexibility and advantages of CP/M combined with high hardware reliability. You will also want a system that takes little space.

Several unified systems have been designed to use CP/M but not the S-100 bus. These include Digital Microsystems, Altos, and others. Often the entire processor, memory, and disk controller are on a single board. This reduces cost, improves reliability, and is more compact. Some of these systems include advanced features not found on other CP/M systems.

The disadvantage of these systems is the loss of flexibility and the inability to update the system as new hardware is available. The system can only be updated by selling it and buying another.

THE MODIFIED SYSTEM ALTERNATIVE

If you purchase a TRS-80, a machine whose basic system does not support CP/M, you may discover that Experimental Research, Inc. supplies a CP/M application program that is just what you need. The program is sold only for CP/M machines, and your system cannot use it.

Don't despair! Several companies have modified CP/M to work with systems that were not originally designed to use CP/M. Examples of systems for which special versions of CP/M are available include the Radio Shack TRS-80 Models I, II, and III; the Northstar Horizon; and the Heath H-8 and H-89. Chances are you won't want to use CP/M on a regular basis with these systems, but having a copy for your system will mean you can use the many available CP/M application programs.

Some of these special versions of CP/M have modifications which make them incompatible with software distributed in the standard CP/M format. The Radio Shack TRS-80, for example, has read-only-memory where CP/M needs read/write memory. This means tricking the processor address lines (as Thinker Toy has done), or loading CP/M in another area of memory. The ROM can become *lost* memory, reducing the available memory for programs. Certain CP/M application programs have to be modified to run on the Radio Shack systems. If you have a system which runs a modified version of CP/M, be sure that the application program you want to run is available for your particular system.

VIDEO TERMINALS

While the processor, disk, and memory are generally sold as a single unit, some type of keyboard and display device must be added to begin using CP/M. This normally some type of video terminal consisting of a video screen, keyboard, and associated electronics. These terminals can be either of two types: serial video terminal or video-mapped display and keyboard.

The serial video terminal is the preferred approach for most business systems. The keyboard and video display is a single unit with the necessary support electronics. Connection is made to the computer with a small multi-wire cable. The connection definition, called RS-232C, is standard between manufacturers.

This permits using just about any serial video terminal with CP/M. The screen generally displays up to 24 lines of 80 characters per line. The screen image is stored in the video terminal's memory, and special character generator circuits interpret the incoming information from the computer and generate the necessary screen characters from the information. Video terminals costs range from $500 to $4,000.

Several questions to explore in shopping for a video terminal are:

1. Does the terminal have upper and lower case? Do the lower case letters have *tails* that descend below the line?
2. What are the baud rates of the terminal? Can the computer transmit and receive at these baud rates?
3. Are the characters clear, sharp, and readable?
4. Is the screen glare-free?
5. Is the keyboard typewriter or teletype styled?
6. Does the keyboard have a positive feel?
7. Does the keyboard have a separate numeric keypad? Is this necessary for your application?
8. Does the terminal have an addressable cursor? The cursor indicates where the next character will be written on the screen. Some application programs require this capability.

The video-mapped display and keyboard combination is generally a lower-cost alternative to the video terminal, but it has some limitations. The keyboard is a separate unit, and a special interface is required to connect the computer to a quality television monitor. The screen image is stored in the computer memory and the character generation is done with circuits on the video interface board, software, or a combination of the two. Such systems have graphics and animation capability, but limited capability as word processors. Most television monitors can only display 12-16 lines of 64 or less characters per line.

The keyboard/display alternative is low cost for applications where high resolution is not needed. Many educational, simulation, and gaming applications fall into this class. Higher resolution systems are available at higher cost. For certain graphic applications the higher cost may be worth it.

PRINTERS

Printers for microsystems can generally be divided into two classes. One class is the dot-matrix printer and the second is the high-quality impact printer that uses a selectric element, daisy wheel, or print thimble.

The dot-matrix printer is the faster type, but the quality is normally not adequate for word processing. The dot-matrix printer is useful for mailing labels, accounting, and volume printing at high reliability. Prices start at $1,000 or less, and the well established dot-matrix printers as the TI 810 are real computer work-horses.

The printers with high print quality use selectric elements, daisy wheels, or removable thimbles. At the low cost end, a used heavy-duty selectric printer with well-designed electronics (as the Anderson/Jacobson) can give reliable service for years at a purchase price of $1,200. We had a similar type of selectric terminal run months of heavy duty usage with no down-time. Printing speed is 15 characters a second. Avoid the office selectrics that have been converted. If you have more money, you will find the Qume, NEC, and Diablo printers will give 45 or 55 characters a second of higher quality printing for about $3,000.

Several considerations are involved in printer selection. In addition to the type of printer, you should explore:

1. How reliable is the printer? Has it been on the market a while and is it well established?
2. What is the throughput speed? This is more than just the printing speed.
3. Can it print a full 132 character line without condensing characters? Is this necessary in your application?
4. Can it print upper and lower case characters?
5. Is the printout very readable?
6. Can it make multiple copies?
7. Are the fonts interchangeable?
8. Can it print bi-directionally?
9. Does it have tractor-feed options?
10. Is a keyboard necessary?
11. Is the interface serial or parallel? Which do you need with your computer?

EXERCISES

1. What are the three basic types of CP/M systems?
2. What are the two basic types of video terminals?
3. What are the two basic types of printers?

CHAPTER 4

Your First CP/M Session

NOTE: This chapter assumes the master CP/M diskette
you receive with your systems is designed specifically for your hardware. If this is not true in your
case, you should get your salesman to create this
type of master. We will also assume the blank
disk referred to in Step 4 is already formatted. If
not, your salesman will need to show you how
the formatting is done on your system. The terms
disk and **diskette** both refer to the floppy disk(s)
used for program and data storage; they are used
interchangably. **Disk drive** is used to refer to the
actual disk system hardware.

CREATING THE BACK-UP COPIES

Your first objective with your computer system should be to
create at least two copies of the master diskette and store one of
these with the master in a safe place. The temptation is to start
experimenting immediately with the master. Don't! Create the
copies first, and experiment with the second one you copy.
Don't take the chance that a hardware failure or your learning
mistake could destroy your master — I've seen it happen!

Now, to create those copies:

Step 1: Turn your system on and load the master diskette
in the system A disk drive. The A drive should be
labelled. If not, see your user manual. If the disk
drive has a door, close this door.

Step 2: Depending upon your system, press *Reset*, *Run*, or *Start*. The disk head should load and a message such as:

```
TARBELL 48K CPM V1.4 of 5-24-78
2SIO FAST SEEK DUAL VERSION>
HOW MANY DISKS? 2
A>
```

should appear on your console. The message differs between systems, but will probably give the CP/M version number, the date CP/M was last changed and the memory size for which this CP/M version was created. It should, at the very least, display an *A*. If the message fails to appear, see Appendix A. If it asks for the number of disks, enter the number of disk drives in your system, i.e., 2 if you have a dual drive system.

Step 3: Type *DIR* and a carriage return. You should see a list of the contents of the disk similar to:

```
A>DIR
A: CPM       COM
A: PIP       COM
A: SUBMIT    COM
A: ED        COM
A: ASM       COM
A: DDT       COM
A: LOAD      COM
A: STAT      COM
A: SYSGEN    COM
A: DUMP      COM
A: COPY      COM
A: PRINT     COM
A: FBIOS24   ASM
A: FBIOS24   PRN
A: FORMAT    COM
A: FBIOS24   HEX
A: FBOOT24   PRN
A: FBOOT24   HEX
A: FBIOS24   BAK
A: FORMAT    ASM
```

```
A: COPY        ASM
A: FBOOT24     ASM
A: CPM47       COM
A: DISKTEST    ASM
A >
```

The list of names will vary depending upon who sold you the master, but the format should be similar to this.

Step 4: Load a blank diskette into the system B disk drive. Type *SYSGEN*. The program will ask for the source disk drive (see Figure 3). Type *A* . The program will now ask for the destination disk drive. Type *B*. The transfer will take only a few seconds, and then the program will request a reboot. Type a carriage return. You have now installed CP/M on the new diskette in Unit B. If you had any problems with this, remove the master and then start your diagnostic work (see Appendix D). Don't use the master disk for diagnostics.

```
A>SYSGEN

SYSGEN VER 1.4
SOURCE DRIVE NAME (OR RETURN TO SKIP)A
SOURCE ON A, THEN TYPE RETURN

FUNCTION COMPLETE
DESTINATION DRIVE NAME (OR RETURN TO REBOOT)B
DESTINATION ON B, THEN TYPE RETURN

FUNCTION COMPLETE
DESTINATION DRIVE NAME (OR RETURN TO REBOOT)

A>
```

Figure 3. System generation

Step 5: Now the files on the master need to be copied onto the diskette in Unit B. With the master still in Unit A type:

pip B: = a:*·*[vo]

This will copy each file from the disk in drive A to the disk in drive B and verify each file by comparing the copied file on B with the original. This will take fifteen or twenty minutes, depending upon the number of files on the Unit A master. The terminal will display the name of each file as it is copied. If any errors are made, an error message will be displayed and the copying will stop. If this happens you should remove the master disk and find out what is wrong with the system before continuing.

Step 6: If there were no errors, you have now created a copy of the master diskette. Remove the diskette from Unit B and label it using a felt pen with a Digital Research Copyright notice and serial number. Remove the master from Unit A and put it in a safe place. It will not be needed again.

Step 7: Now put your newly created diskette in Unit A. Reset and restart. CP/M should come up. Type the number of disks if necessary and *DIR*. Again, you should see the program list on your newly-created diskette.

Step 8: Put another blank diskette in Unit B and repeat steps 4 and 5. This will create a second master. Label this one as before with the copyright notice and serial number.

Step 9: Remove the diskette from Unit A. This is the *father* diskette. The diskette in Unit B is the *son* diskette. Place the *son* diskette from Unit B in Unit A. Re-boot the system and type *DIR* to verify that it copied correctly.

Step 10: Store the purchased master diskette, which is now the *grandfather* with the *father* in a safe place such as your bank safety deposit box. The *son*

diskette becomes your working master for all of
your work from this point. Use it to create additional copies with which to experiment. In emer-
gencies, you could use the father diskette. You
should never need to use the grandfather diskette.

Software is generally not protected in insurance claims. A
friend of ours had an unexpected visitor one evening that used a
fire extinguisher to spray all of his diskettes. The damage was
not covered by his insurance. The moral here is to be sure your
masters are stored at a separate geographic location. This
backup procedure should be followed for every software
package you purchase or develop.

WHAT DOES THE BOOTSTRAP REALLY DO?

A bootstrap is a short computer program used to load
another, larger program. Without the bootstrap, you would
have to sit down and load CP/M into the computer by hand
through some front panel switches—a laborious and time con-
suming job. If the bootstrap program is in the computer
memory, it has the job of loading CP/M from the floppy
diskette where it is stored. This still means you would have the
job of loading the bootstrap manually from front panel
switches, but the bootstrap would be much, much shorter.

The computer manufacturers save us even this trouble by put-
ting the bootstrap in a small read-only-memory chip in the computer. When the computer is first switched on, this memory
overrides a few locations of the normal memory. After CP/M is
loaded, the bootstrap is switched out and the normal memory is
restored. With most systems, the bootstrap is again active
whenever the reset is pressed.

This bootstrap, however, cannot be altered by manufacturers
for various hardware configurations and memory sizes.
Remember, CP/M loads to the highest part of the computer
memory. Where it loads CP/M would depend on the memory
size. To resolve these problems, the bootstrap loader loads
another bootstrap, called a **cold start loader** to the lower part of
the computer memory. This cold start loader is loaded from
Track 0 of the CP/M diskette to the lower part of the computer
memory. This loader can easily be altered for different memory

and hardware configurations. The cold start loader then loads
CP/M to the upper part of the computer memory (see Figure 4).

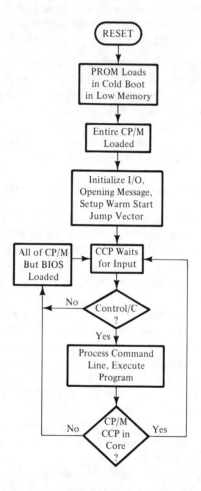

Figure 4. CP/M loading diagram

Both the bootstrap and the loader are very short, and neither
has any error messages to prompt the user. If a problem occurs
on loading CP/M, the loading will terminate with no error
message or prompt. This means it is important to understand
what is happening during the bootstrap so that you can pin-
point the cause in the event of problems. Use Appendix D if you
experience problems.

CORRECTIONS AND CHANGES —
THE CONTROL CODE USE

When entering CP/M commands you will undoubtedly make mistakes and need to correct keyboard entries. The **control key** (normally CNTL or CTRL on the terminal keyboard) is used for corrections and other system control purposes. Simply hold the control key down and press the desired character:

Control/U   Erase the entire line for re-entry.

Control/X   Erase the entire line for re-entry.

Rubout   Erase the last character typed.

Control/H   Erase the last character typed.

Control/C   Reload all of CP/M except the BIOS module.

Control/S   Freeze the console temporarily. Typing any character will resume display.

Control/P   Switches output to both console and printer. Another control/p switches output back to console only.

Control/R   Displays current line in buffer.

Note that rubout does not use the control key. As an exercise, type a line with sevral errors and use the rubout key to correct these errors. Before hitting the carriage return, type a control/r. This will display the line as it currently *looks* to the computer. It can still be corrected (rubout or control/u) and edited. When all corrections are made to the line, then type the carriage return.

The Control/S permits viewing data when the console is set for high baud rates. Type a *DIR* command and while the display is scrolling type the Control/S. The display will freeze, and then resume as soon as you type anothe character.

EXERCISES

1. Give at least two reasons why a double-level bootstrap is used with CP/M.
2. Why would a normal selectric keyboard be difficult to use as an input for CP/M?
3. Why are dual disks generally considered the minimum disk configuration?

CHAPTER 5

Files, Records, and Disks

RECORDS, FILES, SECTORS, AND TRACKS

In this chapter we will discuss the organization of data within the CP/M file system. Various systems use a variety of diskette sizes and densities, but by far the most common is the single sided, eight inch, single density diskette. These diskettes, conforming to the IBM 3740 flexible disk standard, are what are normally referred to as *CP/M compatible* diskettes. The rest of the chapter discusses this format. Consult your user manual for formats which are unique to your system.

The eight inch single-density floppy disk often used with CP/M has 77 **"physical" tracks** of 26 sectors each. Each **sector** can store 128 bytes along with some extra bytes for error-checking purposes (CRC information). This gives a total disk capacity of slightly over 256,000 usable bytes. I used the quotes with the term *physical* because you cannot actually see the tracks or the sectors. Each track is a separate physical entity magnetically imprinted on the diskette. The individual tracks are made up of sectors. CP/M accesses data stored on the diskette by reading and writing the tracks and sectors on the diskette.

CP/M can only access sector quantities from the diskette tracks. It cannot read half a sector or three quarters of a sector, but always one or more sectors. All sectors are equal length and exactly 128 bytes (or characters long). Other disk systems may use different size floppies, a different number of tracks and sectors, or a different recording density; but the disk will always be addressed in sector-like entities. If your system is a double density system, each sector is 256 bytes.

Now the chances are you are interested in storing information of varying lengths for various applications. An information entity is called a **record**. A record is a collection of related items treated as a unit. It could be an English sentence, three numbers, one number or a series of thirty names. What is important is that you see these items as a unit or single entity. A **file** is a collection of related records treated as a single item. Records and files are logical information divisions.

The distinction between logical and physical storage is important. The information is stored on the disk as physical sectors and tracks. The user sees information as logical records and files. Tracks and sectors are always the same length. Records and files may be of varying length (see Figure 5).

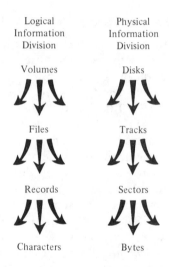

Logical Information Division — Physical Information Division

Volumes — Disks

Files — Tracks

Records — Sectors

Characters — Bytes

Figure 5. Logical and physical information division

Since records are logically separated, it is the software (your program) that recognizes where one record ends and the next begins. The Editor, for example, uses a carriage return to separate records. The common input statement in BASIC assumes carriage returns, commas, and other special characters separate records. If a BASIC LINE INPUT statement is used for input, the BASIC will assume records to be separated by carriage returns only. The character(s) used to define record separation is (are) called a delimiter(s) (see Figure 6).

Editor	Carriage return
BASIC "Input" statement	Carriage returns, commas, and special characters
BASIC "line-input" statement	Carriage return

Figure 6. Record separators

You, as the user, need never concern yourself with where things are stored on the diskette (sector, track, etc.). CP/M takes care of all of this. You are only interested in records and files, and your programs will access data from the diskette as records and files. When you type *DIR*, you will see the list of the files on the diskette currently mounted in the disk drive, but that doesn't mean the disk files are stored in that sequential order. Pieces and portions of each file may be located at various places on the disk.

FILE NAMES

Using a *DIR* command, you will get a list of the files stored on the disk. Each file name consists of two parts: a primary file name and a file type.

The **file type** consists of one to three characters and defines the class of the file. Examples would be:

BAS   basic program file

COM   machine language program file

ASM   assembly level source program

HEX   a program in INTEL hex format

ASC   ASCII character data file

INT   intermediate language file

BAK   back-up editor file

FOR   fortran source file

PRN   compiled print listings

$$$ temporary files

Files with the same file type are normally processed in the same way. In some cases you are free to choose your own file type, but in most cases you are not. In using BASIC or the assembler, for example, it is necessary to use the correct file type. The BASIC interpreter or the assembler looks for the file type and, if a file name of that type is not found, an error will result.

The primary file name consists of one to eight characters. All of the keyboard characters and numbers can be used except:

. , : ; = ? * [ ]

The primary name should be chosen to indicate something unique about the file. For example, a general ledger program in BASIC could be named:

LEDGER.BAS

In this case LEDGER is the primary file name and BAS is the file type.

The full file name always consists of the file name and file type separated by a single period. CP/M translates all lower case letters in file names and types to upper case.

FILE REFERENCES

In referencing files on the disk, the user may reference a group or class of files or a single file. In copying a disk, for example, you may want to copy all BASIC programs to a second disk. In this case the copying command would want to reference all *BAS* type files. If a reference implies only a single file on the disk it is called an *unambiguous file* (or ufn) reference. Examples would be:

FB10S24.ASM

MBASIC.COM

LOAD.COM

If the reference implies more than one file on the disk, it is called an *ambiguous file* (afn) reference. This is done by using a *?* in the file reference to indicate which characters need not be matched to satisfy the file reference. For example the reference:

?BASIC.COM

would refer to MBASIC.COM, CBASIC.COM and EBASIC.COM. If all three of these files are on a diskette and the copying operation referenced ?BASIC.COM, all three files would be copied. Any number of question marks can be used in the reference as:

MAIL.???

to reference files with a name of MAIL and any type, such as MAIL.BAS and MAIL.INT.

A single asterisk may be used to reference a group of files with the same file name or file type. It can be used as a substitute for a group of question marks. For example:

*.BAS

would reference all files type BAS on the disk and:

FB10S24.*

would reference all the files with file name FB10S24 such as FB10S24.ASM, FB10S24.PRN, and FB10S.HEX, and FB10S24.COM.

Both ambiguous and unambiguous file references can be used in many commands referencing files as:

A>DIR *.BAS

would list all BASIC files on the disk.

OPENING AND CLOSING FILES

Before a file can be used it must be *opened* and, when the file is no longer to be used, it is *closed* and released. When a file is opened, certain directory information (file indexes) are moved to the computer memory and a buffer for the disk information is created in the computer memory. As the file is updated this directory information in the computer is updated and whenever the buffer is full it is written to the disk. After the file is updated, the last bit of information entered to the file is probably still in the buffer. Filling up the buffer does not automatically cause it to be written to the disk, and if you remove the disk or turn the computer off that information will be lost. By *closing* the file, the last data in the buffer is written to the disk and the directory is updated to index the new updated file. If power is lost on the system before the file is closed, some of your information will be lost, but the directory and file information will always correspond unless you lost power at the exact moment the computer was writing the new directory update.

Files should always be closed before shutting the system down or changing disks. Most application programs close files automatically or provide commands to allow you to close them. In BASIC a *close* command will move the remainder of the data buffer to the output files. In the Editor this is done with the *E* command.

With input files, it is not necessary to be so careful about closing files. An input file is never updated, so the directory is not changed and the *close* command only releases the computer space for another *open* command.

DISK SELECTION

CP/M addresses up to four disk drives with drive designations of Unit A, Unit B, Unit C, and Unit D. The bootstrap always loads CP/M from Unit A. Programs and files can be loaded from any of the active disks. Most systems only use disks A and B.

When CP/M first comes up, it will prompt the operator with a *A*>. This indicates that if you do not specify any disk drive (as when you loaded SYSGEN to create your backups), CP/M will assume the program (SYSGEN in this case) is to come from the *A* unit. Drive Unit A is referred to as the *logged on* disk, and as such is the default drive for all activity if no other disk unit is specified. You can change the default drive at any time by specifying the new drive with a colon and carriage return as:

A>B: (carriage return)

Then the *B* disk will be *logged on* and the console will indicate this with:

B>

All files referenced without a drive name will now be from the B drive. The prompt character always indicates the currently logged on disk.

BUILT-IN COMMANDS

There are five commands built into the CCP module. These are referred to as the **built-in** commands. You have already used one of these (DIR) to obtain a directory of the files on a disk. The other four are

ERA (erases file)   SAVE (saves file)

REN (renames file)   TYPE (types file)

Remember that CP/M translates all lower case commands to upper case, so if your terminal has lower case it is not necessary to type any of these commands in upper case.

The DIR Command

The DIR command is used for listing the files on a disk. It can be used without any file references (as you have discovered already) to list all the files on the disk. It can also be used with an ambiguous file reference to list all the files satisfying a particular classification. For example, to list all BASIC files on the disk type:

A>DIR *.BAS (Carriage return)

The ambiguous file references can also be proceeded by a drive name and colon. This will cause the directory listing of the named file as:

A>DIR B:*.*

If there are no files on the disk the directory will be empty and the DIR command will type:

NOT FOUND

A directory request on a new or blank diskette will give the same message. If a disk is SYSGENed with CP/M, the directory is not changed and no files are lost.

A printout of the disk directory can be made by doing a control/P just before the carriage return. After the disk directory is printed, another control/P will stop the printer. It is a good idea to give each of your disks a unique number and a unique subject area (as *games*, *General Ledger*, etc.) and keep a printed directory of each disk in a special notebook.

The directory is stored on Track 3 of the disk. Physical damage to track three can destroy the directory, making the disk essentially useless. Although it is possible to recover information from a disk without the directory, it is a lengthy and complex process. Damaged files can be copied to another disk and corrected, but a damaged directory means the pointers or index to these files are lost. Finding information on the disk without the directory would be similar to trying to find a word or phrase in a book without an index. Techniques to do this require some skill in programming.

The ERA Command

The ERA command erases files from disks. It can be used with an unambiguous or ambiguous file reference as:

ERA MAIL.BAS (carriage return) (erases MAIL.BAS)

ERA *.BAS (carriage return) (erases all BAS files on disk)

The command can be used to erase all files on the currently logged on disk by typing:

ERA *.* (carriage return)

In this case you will get a prompt:

ALL FILES (Y/N)?

which requires a *Y* response before the files are removed.

Files can be removed on disks that are not currently logged-on by using the drive designator with a colon before the file name as:

A>ERA B:*.PRN (carriage return)

This removes all PRN files on Unit B. Disk A remains logged on.

Erasing the files on a disk releases the space for other files, so files that are no longer useful should always be erased. You should also be aware that once a file is erased it ceases to exist. Although it may be possible, it is difficult to recover the file or use it again.

The REN Command

The REN command is used to change disk file names. In contrast to the DIR and ERA command, REN always references an unambiguous file (always refers to a single, unique file). The form of the command is:

A>REN ufn1 = ufn2 (carriage return)

where unf1 is the complete new file name (file name and file type) and ufn2 is the complete old file name (file name and file type). The two names are separated by an equal sign or an arrow pointing to the left. Examples:

A>REN TEST.ASM = TEST.BAK (carriage return)

A>REN RFLEE.ASC = RFLE.ASC (carriage return)

A>REN TASK.BAS = TASK.ASC (carriage return)

After renaming, there is no longer any file on the disk with the old file name.

The file name can be preceded by a disk drive unit name to reference a file on a specific disk unit as:

A>REN PROCESS.BAS = B:TEST.BAS (carriage return)

A>REN A:MAIL.BAS = TEST.BAS (carriage return)

The rename command does not copy any files to any disk, but only renames them. Hence, ufn1 and unf2 must be on the same disk. Either, both, either or neither file name may be proceeded by a drive name, but if both file names are preceded by a drive name the drives must be identical. For example:

A>REN A.MAIL.BAS = B:MAIL.BAS (carriage return)

would not be a legal command. Remember, REN references a single file.

If uf2 cannot be found to rename, the console will display

NOT FOUND

If uf1 already exists on a disk, renaming another file to this would give a duplicate file name; therefore, if uf1 already exists the message:

FILE EXISTS

will be displayed and the rename will not be performed.

The SAVE Command

The SAVE command *lifts* the contents of the transient program area from the computer memory and stores it in a file on a floppy disk. An unambiguous file name must be specified for the stored file. In addition, you must also specify the number of 256 byte pages that are saved from the transient program area as:

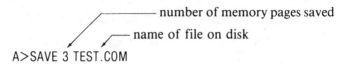

number of memory pages saved

name of file on disk

A>SAVE 3 TEST.COM

Remember, the transient program area begins with the second page of memory (location 100H), and CP/M programs always start at this second page. The SAVE command saves from the second page onward for the number of pages specified.

A disk drive can also be specified with the file name as:

A>SAVE 32 B:WHAT.COM

This command is useful in saving a program running in memory if you have temporarily modified it. The program can later be reloaded directly from memory and run.

It is often useful to use the DDT utility and SAVE commands to make minor modifications in a program without having to go through a re-assembly process.

The TYPE Command

The TYPE command is useful for scanning and examining a file already on disk. It is quick and easy to use. For example, if you see a strange file name on the disk and you are curious as to what is in the file, use the TYPE command to examine the file. The command, however, is only useful with ASCII files — that is, files written in normal alphabetic and numeric characters. A TYPE on a machine level program would be meaningless. BASIC programs for CBASIC can be scanned with the TYPE command as well as Microsoft BASIC programs if they were saved with the ASCII option. Files set up with the Editor can also be scanned with the TYPE command. To use, simply type the command and an unambiguous file reference as:

A>TYPE LEDGER.BAS (carriage return)

Disk drive names can also be included as:

A>TYPE B:MAIL.BAS (carriage return)

If the command scans the file too fast, use the control/S to freeze the display momentarily. Striking any key again will resume the scan.

This type command can also be used to type a file on the printer by using a control/P just before the carriage return as:

A>TYPE LEDGER.BAS (control/P, carriage return)

EXERCISES

1. Define the following:

    sector   record
    track   file

2. How many files can be stored on a CP/M disk?
3. What is meant by opening a file? Closing a file? What happens if the computer is stopped and the disks removed without closing the files in use?
4. List the CP/M built-in commands and briefly describe each.

CHAPTER 6

Using the Utilities

Several programs are included with your CP/M system that can be loaded to the transient program area and run as any other program. The programs, called **utilities**, are used to perform many commonly required functions. The programs are proprietary, and you don't get the source file (ASM file) for these. They reside on your CP/M disk as COM files, and can be called by name. The utilities include:

ED	CP/M editor
PIP	Peripheral interchange program
DDT	Dynamic debugger
STAT	Disk and file status
ASM	Assembler for source level programs
SYSGEN	Generates a new CP/M on a diskette
DUMP	Dump a disk file (source for this program is in CP/M manuals)
MOVCPM	Modifies CP/M system
SUBMIT	Permits batch program operation
LOAD	Converts the output program of the assembler (HEX file) to a machine level format (COM file)

Only three of these will be discussed in this chapter.

Any COM program can be loaded and run without using the file type as:

> A>PIP (carriage return)

This command would automatically load the program PIP.COM and run it.

DISK READ/WRITE STATUS

Before getting into the utilities themselves, it is important to understand a common problem area in the CP/M file system. Sometimes in trying to write a file you may get the aggravating message:

BDOS ERR ON A: R/O

To prevent this from occurring you need to understand how CP/M treats disk directory and file status information.

When a disk is being used, part of its directory information is in the computer memory. If you change disks, this information no longer matches the disk you are using and any files written to disk using this information in memory would be scrambled. To protect against this, whenever the disk is changed the CP/M recognizes this and will not let you write to the new disk until a warm start (control/C) or reboot is done. This forces a read of the new disk directory and allows you to write to the new disk. As a precaution, *always* do a control/C or reboot when loading a new disk. If you are using a BASIC interpreter and need to change disks, most BASICs have a command (RESET) that will force a directory read of the new disk.

THE DUMP UTILITY

The CP/M DUMP utility is used to view or print the contents of a disk file. The command form for using the program is:

A>DUMP xxx.yyy (carriage return)

where xxx.yyy is the name of the file to dump. The output will be displayed in hexadecimal form, sixteen bytes per line. The source listing of this program is used as an example in the *CP/M Interface Guide*. Enhanced versions of this program are available from several manufacturers, including the CP/M User's Group.

TRANSFERRING FILES – USING THE PIP UTILITY

PIP is the program abbreviation for CP/M's peripheral interchange program. This program is used to copy a file from one disk to another (or to another place on the same disk), to merge files together, to copy a file from the disk to the printer, or to support a variety of file transfers between input and output devices. Several parameters are available for file modification during the transfer process.

The PIP program (see Figure 7) transfers information from one or more sources to a single destination. Typical applications include:

1. Copying a file to another disk for back-up purposes.
2. Printing a file on the printer.
3. Merging two or more files to a single file.
4. Storing input information (paper tape, modem input, or a serial input file from another computer) on the disk.
5. Outputting a file to another computer, modem, or paper punch.

If the output is to a disk file, output operation is always temporarily to a .$$$ file. If the transfer is successful, the output file is renamed to the name of the destination file. This two step process is used to ensure that a good copy has been made before deleting any old files with the same name as the specified destination file.

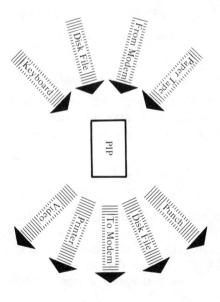

Figure 7. PIP information flow

Calling up PIP

PIP can be called in either of two ways:

1. A>PIP (carriage return)

2. A>PIP t1, t2, t3,----tn (carriage return)

In the first case PIP is loaded into the transient program area and begins execution by displaying an asterisk. One or more transfer commands are then entered, separated by commas, and terminated with a carriage return.

Example:

A>PIP

*X.BAS = Y.BAS, NEW.BAS = OLD.BAS (carriage return)

*MAIL.BAS = TEST.BAS (carriage return)

The transfer will be initiated immediately after the carriage return. After the transfer is complete PIP will display an asterisk again. To return to the CP/M monitor, input a carriage return only (an empty line) or use the control/C.

In the second case PIP is loaded and will immediately begin executing the transfer commands, starting from left (t1) to right (tn).

The form of the transfer command is the same in either case:

$$destination = source$$

or

$$destination = source \#1, source \#2, ----source \#n$$

Either the destination or source names, if disk files, can be preceded by the disk drive name and colon. If no disk drive is specified, the currently logged disk is assumed.

Examples:

A>PIP B:MAIL.BAS = A:MAIL.BAS

A>PIP A:MAD.ASC = MADT.ASC

In the first case the file MAIL.BAS is duplicated on the B disk and the file on the A disk is unaltered. In the second case, a second file called MAD.ASC is created on the A disk that is identical to MADT.ASC on the same disk.

The same file name may appear as both a source and destination as:

A>.BUILD.ASM = BUILD1.ASM, BUILD.ASM

In this case BUILD1.ASM and BUILD.ASM are merged to a temporary output .$$$ file. After the transfer if the transfer is successful the PIP will rename the .$$$ file to BUILD.ASM and the original BUILD.ASM file is lost (erased). If the transfer is not successful (an error condition), the original files will not be lost.

If a PIP transfer ever ends prematurely for some reason (as if you ran out of disk space), you may see this temporary .$$$ file on the disk with a directory listing. A scan of this file (using the TYPE command) may give the illusion it is your output file, but check it carefully. The end of the file may be missing! The problem should be corrected (STAT), PIP restarted, and the transfer done again. For this reason it is generally not wise to use the same file name as both a source and destination file if you are copying to the same disk.

Non-Disk Sources and Destination

Files can be transferred to or from any peripheral in the system using either the physical or logical device name for the peripheral. For example, to print file TEST.BAS you could enter:

A>PIP LST: = TEST.BAS (carriage return)

The destination of the file is controlled from the BIOS software driver. If the LIST driver in the BIOS software is set up (physically) for the printer, either LST: or LPT: will output to the printer. Other names and device codes can also be used and are described in *An Introduction to CP/M Features and Facilities*. (A file print can also be done with TYPE.)

PIP Abbreviated Commands

If the source and destination files have the same name, it is only necessary to use the name once.

For example:

A>PIP OUTPUT.FOR = B:[v] (carriage return)

copies the OUTPUT.FOR to A (the currently logged disk) from B and verifies the transfer. This abbreviated form can only be used in transferring files between disks and when the files have identical names.

Unambiguous file names can also be used as:

A>PIP B: = *.* [vo] (carriage return)

transfers all files from the disk in drive A to the disk in drive B and verifies each transfer. In transferring unambiguous files, each file is listed on the console as it is copied. The parameters *vo* will be explained in the next section.

PIP Parameter Control

It is also possible to pass parameters to PIP to control the transfer or modify the file as it is transferred from the source to the destination. As an example, the command:

A>PIP LST: = B:RFLE.ASC [L] (carriage return)

will print out the file RFLE.ASC, translating all upper case characters to lower case. The full list of parameter controls is shown in Table 1. Parameters can be combined as desired. For example, the command:

A>PIP LST: = B:RFLE.ASC [LT8] (carriage return)

will print the RFLE.ASC file, changing upper case to lower case and converting all tabs to eight spaces. Source disk files are not changed.

The verify command [vo] should be used in copying all disk files to insure the file is copied correctly. The object file parameter (o) should be used in transferring all files that are not character strings. This includes all CBASIC.INT files and MBASIC files.

Examples:

A>PIP CRT: = B:TEXT.ASC [T8] (carriage return)

A>PIP B:SUBFLE.ASC = FILE.ASC [VO] (carriage return)

Copying Programs with PIP

Remember with CP/M you cannot change the diskette in a drive without doing a control/C. This can create problems in a dual disk system unless PIP is used correctly. Suppose, for example, PIP is on your diskette volume #7 and you want to copy a program from volume 10 to volume 11. Here is your procedure:

1. Load diskette #7 into drive A and load diskette #11 into drive B.
2. Type PIP (carriage return) to load PIP to the transient program area.

3. Remove diskette #7 from drive A and insert diskette #10 in drive A. Although you have changed the diskette in drive A, you can still read (but not write to) this drive.
4. Now give the necessary PIP command to copy the file or files from drive A (diskette #10) to drive B (diskette #11).

Parameter	Function
B	Block mode transfer. Data is retained in the computer memory until a control/s is received. The memory is then cleared and returns for more data.
Dn	Deletes any charactrs beyond the nth character in the transfer.
E	Echo all transferred characters to the console.
F	Remove all form feeds in the transfer.
H	Hex data transfer. Data is checked for hex character format for Intel systems.
I	Ignore ":00" records in an Intel hex transfer.
L	Translate upper characters to lower case in the transfer.
N	Add line numbers to each line transferred, starting at one and incrementing by one.
O	Object file transfer (non-ASCII). All control/z characters are not interpreted as end-of-file.
Pn	Add page ejects every n lines.
Qs↑z	Quit copying when the string "s" is found.
Ss↑z	Start copying when the string "s" is found.
Tn	Convert tabs to n spaces.
U	Convert lower case letters to upper case on the transfer.
V	Verify the file copies correctly by comparing the copied file with the original.
Z	Zero the left-most bit on each transferred ASCII character. This is normally a parity bit.

Table 1. PIP Parameters

THE STAT PROGRAM

STAT is a CP/M program that provides the user with information as to how much space each file uses and how much space is left on the disk. This program varies considerably between manufacturers, as many manufacturers rewrite this or provide their own status program with different features from the CP/M version. The description here includes the CP/M version 1.4 only.

An Exercise with STAT

Mount a disk in your system and bring up the CP/M. Then enter the following command:

A>STAT A:*.* (carriage return)

With a Tarbell CP/M disk, you might get the following directory and printout:

RECS	BYTS	EX	D:FILENAME.TYP
64	8K	1	A:ASM.COM
66	9K	1	A:COPY.ASM
60	8K	1	A:COPY.COM
1	1K	1	A:CORRES.ASC
70	9K	1	A:CPM.COM
64	8K	1	A:CPM47.COM
38	5K	1	A:DDT.COM
152	19K	2	A:DISKTEST.ASM
4	1K	1	A:DUMP.COM
48	6K	1	A:ED.COM
209	27K	2	A:FBIOS24.ASM
25	4K	1	A:FBIOS24.HEX
344	43K	3	A:FBIOS24.PRN
16	2K	1	A:FBOOT24.ASM
3	1K	1	A:FBOOT24.HEX
26	4K	1	A:FBOOT24.PRN
59	8K	1	A:FORMAT.ASM
4	1K	1	A:FORMAT.COM
0	0K	1	A:LETTER.BAK
2	1K	1	A:LETTER.LIB
14	2K	1	A:LOAD.COM
55	7K	1	A:PIP.COM

```
    4    1K    1    A:PRINT.COM
   24    3K    1    A:STAT.COM
   10    2K    1    A:SUBMT.COM
    8    1K    1    A:SYSGEN.COM
    3    1K    1    A:TEST.ASC
    0    0K    1    A:TEST.ASM
   26   16K    1    A:X$$$$$$$.LIB
BYTES REMAINING ON A: 59K

A>
```

If the program doesn't run or you get the message:

STAT?

This means STAT isn't on this disk. Use PIP to move it from another disk or try this exercise with a disk containing STAT.

Notice that the listing shows the files in alphabetical order. The order in which the files are printed has no relationship as to how they are stored on the disk. You have *no* information on where or how the files are stored on the disk — nor do you need it. With CP/M you access files by name — not by physical location.

The first number indicates the number of physical sectors used by the file. Each sector can store 128 bytes on a low-density 8″ disk. There are 73 usable tracks, with each track containing 26 sectors. This gives 242,944 bytes of usable storage in the standard IBM format.

The second number is the number of bytes used by the file, expressed in kilobytes (1,024 bytes).

$$\#kilobytes = \frac{(\#sectors) \times (128)}{1024}$$

The third number is the number of *extents* or directory entries used by the file. A given directory entry can access 16,384 (16K) bytes of disk space. As a file grows beyond this, CP/M will create an additional directory entry (or *extent*) for each 16K the file uses. A file can have up to 16 extents. A given disk can have up to 64 directory entries.

The remainder of the entry is the file name; both the file name and file type are listed. At the end of the listing the amount of free disk space is given. In some versions of STAT supplied by manufacturers, the null directory entries are listed separately and the number of free directory entries is given.

A user should not expect CP/M to monitor the disk and give appropriate messages when the disks are full. This monitoring is the responsibility of the user program (or, if used, the high-level compiler or interpreter).

The CP/M utility programs all have some level of monitoring on the disk space; and PIP, the assembler, and the editor will all give messages on a full disk — but these are generated from the program, not CP/M. As a safety precaution, use STAT occasionally to monitor your disk space. Most CP/M errors occur due to improper disk handling (not entering control/C when changing disks) or from insufficient disk space for a requested operation. If you get any type of unusual error message, check your disk space first with STAT.

Using STAT for File Storage Information

STAT has several forms and can be used in any of several ways:

STAT *.* (cr) or STAT B:*.*	Gives the full directory and space allocation
STAT *.BAS (cr)	Gives directory information on all files with the specified file type.
STAT (cr)	Storage space available on current active drive and whether each drive is read/write status or read-only (see next section) as: A>STAT A:R/W SPACE: 111K In this case drive A has 111K bytes of space available for use.
STAT B: (cr)	Gives available space on the listed drive only.
STAT B: = R/0 (cr)	Disk B is set to read-only (write protected) until the system is rebooted.

As mentioned earlier, STAT varies considerably from system to system. Check your system's user documentation to get the specific details for your CP/M version.

Device Assignment

In some CP/M systems, STAT can be used to switch output devices. The output that normally goes to the display, for example, can be switched to the printer. This is helpful for documenting a procedure of keeping a full log of an operator's work. Afterwards, STAT is again used to switch the output back to the video. Not all manufacturers implement this CP/M option —check your system manuals. The feature is not critical, as DDT can be used to alter the BIOS to do this by changing a single BIOS instruction. The printer can also be switched on and off with the control/P option.

EXERCISES

1. Can a PIP file name be lower case letters? What will happen if you use lower case letters?
2. Describe what each of the following commands do:

    a. A>PIP B: = *.* [vo] (carriage return)
    b. A>PIP SUB = SLETTER.ASC [STRANS:(control/Z)QL3 (control/z)] (carriage return)
    c. A>PIP TEST.ASM = TEST1.ASM
    d. A>PIP B: = A:*.BAS [vo]
    e. B>PIP LST: = RFLE.ASC [LT8]

3. A file TEST.ASM has page ejects every 60 lines and you wish a file with page ejects every 58 lines. How would you convert the file?
4. You have a file with line numbers in columns 73-80. Define a copy operation to strip the numbers off.
5. What are some of the problems involved in using the PIP program to handle dialogue between a video terminal and another computer using a modem?
6. What is the relationship between the order of the files in a STAT listing and their order on the disk?
7. What is the maximum number of directory entries possible on a CP/M disk? How would large files reduce the number of possible directory entries?
8. What is a utility? List four CP/M utilities.

CHAPTER 7

Back-up Procedures and Disk Care

BACK-UP PROCEDURES

Information stored on a floppy disk has value. It has monetary value, information value, and represents time. If a purchased program, as your general ledger, is destroyed you would have to purchase another. If a mailing list is destroyed, the list would have to be re-entered. In most cases insurance will not cover information that is lost, and it is almost impossible to put a value on your time if you have to rebuild a file.

A diskette properly used and stored will last for years. Most of the problems with lost information occur because of operator errors. Over 90% of file losses on our system are simply user mistakes — a file is copied over the wrong file or a file is accidentally erased. The other 10% of our data losses are from actual physical damage to the disk.

To protect against that inevitable day when you will lose files or disks, you should always create duplicate copies of files and programs, and both should be duplicate copies of files and programs, and both should be duplicated again on updating or correcting. This is called *backing-up the disk*, and is a fundamental rule to the cost-effective management of any computer installation. Always keep at least two copies of everything.

Whenever you purchase a program, always make a verified copy (PIP [vo] option) of the program immediately, then use the copy. The master should be stored in a safe deposit box or at a separate location. Use PIP as follows to create the copy with the *vo* options:

```
PIP B: = A:*.* [vo]
```

As a second rule, if you create a file (as a mailing list file) the file should also be copied to a second disk and verified as it is copied.

Third, if you update or modify a program or data file, back this up again to a second disk and verify using PIP.

Fourth, whenever a source program is purchased or developed, or if you update a source program, maintain a listing of the program in a file. This listing becomes important if you accidentally erase both a back-up file and master file. Other data files, as mailing lists, should also periodically be printed out and saved for the same reason.

Fifth, document your disk files carefully so you can locate information quickly.

BACK-UP DISK RULES

1. Whenever a program is purchased, it should be copied to a second disk before being used and the master never used. The copy operation should be verified.

2. Whenever a file is created, a back-up copy of the file should be created and verified on a second disk.

3. Whenever a file is updated, the back-up copy of the file should be updated and verified.

4. Back-up copies, as much as possible, should be stored in a safety deposit box or at a separate geographic location.

5. Maintain a file of the listings of all source programs. (Note: Some purchased programs will not have source listings).

CARE AND HANDLING OF FLOPPY DISKS

Your disk has value because of the information stored in its magnetic surface. This surface can be damaged easily with improper handling, but with proper handling your information will last indefinitely. Here are some tips to protect these disks:

1. Don't expose your disks to extremes of heat and cold. Keep the disks away from direct sunlight and windows.

2. Don't keep or use disks in a dusty room or near cigarettes.

3. Store disks in their proper envelopes.

4. Store disks vertically or, if in a horizontal pile, no more than ten deep.

5. Handle disks only by their plastic covers. Never touch the media surface.

6. Don't leave disks open and lying about — even temporarily.

7. Never use pencils on disks, as the graphite will ruin the surface and the point pressure can cause damage. Use felt pens, write on the label, and then place the label on the disk.

8. Don't try to clean a floppy disk.

9. Avoid using disks around magnetic fields. If the computer case is plastic, remember magnetic fields from the power supply inside the case can erase a nearby floppy outside the case.

10. Don't put a damaged disk in a drive.

11. Never stack labels on a disk. Use only one label.

12. Disks can be kept continually loaded and rotating, but they will experience more wear at the center hole. In most cases, the disk should be removed when it is not being used.

13. If a disk is mailed, protect it against bending and dust damage.

As a precautionary rule, *always* copy programs and data files to a back-up disk. Check the back-up to be sure it copied correctly.

If your computer has a single step or *halt* button, avoid using it with CP/M, particularly in reading or writing disks. To stop a run-away computer use the control/S. Then use the control/C to get the operating system. Control/S should always give keyboard control again.

CHAPTER 8

The Editor — Introduction

INTRODUCTION

The Editor is a CP/M utility program used to create and modify CP/M ASCII files. ASCII files are those files that consist entirely of alphabetic, numeric, and special characters. The following files normally fall into such classification:

1. Assembly Program source files.
2. Text editing files (correspondence, manuscripts, forms, etc.).
3. BASIC source programs (except Microsoft BASIC files unless saved with Microsoft option *A*).
4. Certain data files used in programs.
5. Most source programs for high-level languages (FOR-TRAN, Pascal, etc.).

The following files are not ASCII files and generally are not (or cannot be) created or modified with the Editor:

1. Machine-level files with COM file type.
2. HEX files created by the assembler.
3. CBASIC intermediate language files (INT file type).
4. Certain BASIC data files.

CALLING THE EDITOR AND BASIC OPERATION

The editor is called by referencing an unambiguous file name as:

```
A>ED filename cr
```

Examples:

A>ED TASK.BAS cr

or

A>ED B:LEDGER.BAS cr

Note that a disk unit may be specified if desired and the file type must be included. Calling the editor:

1. Opens the referenced file for input to the editor program. If the file does not exist, a directory entry is created with the file name and a *NEW FILE* message is generated on the console.
2. Opens an output file with the same file name as the input file and a file type of *$$$* (see Figure 8).
3. Generates an asterisk at the console to indicate the editor is in command mode.

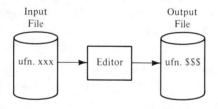

Figure 8. Editor file processing

At this point nothing has been read from the input file to the editor. The input and output files have only been opened. The editor is now waiting for a command from you.

The editor is always in one of two modes. If an asterisk is printed, the editor is in the command mode and waiting for some type of command to be entered. If no asterisk is displayed, the editor is in an input mode waiting for console input data for entry into the output file. When the editor first comes up, it is always in command mode.

Data (sentences, computer programs, alphanumeric characters, etc.) is always processed from the input file to the output file. The editor can make changes, add data, delete data, or otherwise manipulate the data from the input file. If no input file exists, all data in the output file must be created using the editor insert command.

FILE COMMANDS

The editor commands used in the command mode can be grouped into five classes:

1. File commands — open, close, read and write files.
2. Line commands — modify, add, and delete lines of text.
3. Character commands — modify, add, and delete characters within lines.
4. Complex commands — search, move, and repetitive commands.
5. Control commands — sets up control parameters for editor operation.

For our first two sessions, we will use only the file commands, two line commands from class 2, and a search command from class 4. This will give you a feel of the capabilities of the editor. As you gain experience, you can use your CP/M editor manual to learn the other commands.

YOUR FIRST EDITOR SESSION — CREATING A FILE

One of the best ways to begin learning the editor is to sit down and work through a session, then try to find out what you did. So let's start. With a disk containing the editor and some free working space, type:

```
A>ED TEST.ASC (carriage return)
```

The editor will load and the console will display:

```
NEW FILE
   *
```

This indicates that TEST.ASC is not already on the disk. Now type an "*I*" to insert your text and a carriage return:

```
A>ED TEST.ASC (carriage return)
NEW FILE
*I (carriage return)
```

Now type in your text as a normal manuscript with carriage returns, using a lower case as appropriate if your terminal has this option:

```
A>ED TEST.ASC
*I
Now is the time for all good
men to come to the aid of their
country.
```

After you have completed the desired text, type a control/Z. This will put you back in the command mode and the console will display an asterisk. Now type a *B* with a #*T* as:

*B #T

This will begin at the beginning of the file and display the contents of the entire file as:

```
*B #T
NOW IS THE TIME FOR ALL GOOD
MEN TO COME TO THE AID OF THEIR
COUNTRY.
```

Notice that the entire text is now in capital letters. The letters were translated to the upper case by the editor because a capital "*I*" was used before the input. If a lower case "*i*" has been used, the letters would not have been translated to upper case but would have remained as typed. The *B* of this command starts the output from the beginning of the text, and the #*T* indicates all lines are to be displayed.

Now return to the monitor with an *E* as:

*E (carriage return)

Now do a DIR and you will find your new file on the disk:

A>DIR *.ASC

You can also examine it with the TYPE command:

```
A>TYPE TEXT.ASC
NOW IS THE TIME FOR ALL GOOD
MEN TO COME TO THE AID OF THEIR
COUNTRY.
```

Now let's examine how this file was created. On calling up the editor, the file TEST.ASC did not exist. A temporary file was opened on the disk with the name TEST.$$$. The *I* command moved you out of the command mode into the input mode. As you typed the text into the console, it was stored in the computer memory.

After the text had been entered, the control/z took the editor back to the command mode. The *E* command

1. transferred the entire text in the computer memory to the disk,
2. renamed the temporary file to TEST.ASC, and
3. returned the system to the CP/M monitor.

YOUR SECOND EDITOR SESSION — MODIFYING A FILE

Now enter the editor call and the file name as:

A>ED TEXT.ASC (carriage return)

This will load and start the editor, open the TEST.ASC file that was created in the first session, and open a temporary file on the disk with the name TEST.$$$ (see Figure 9). The editor then displays an asterisk on the console indicating that it is in the command mode:

A>ED TEST.ASC (carriage return)
*

Nothing from the file has been read to the computer memory. The files have only been opened. Now read two lines from the disk to the computer memory by entering:

*2A (carriage return)

The *A* is a command abbreviation for **append**, and reads a file or portion of a file from the disk to the computer memory. You will hear the head load on the disk, the two lines of the text will be entered into the computer memory, and the console will again display an asterisk. To view these lines, it is necessary to use the *T* command. To view the entire text currently in the computer memory, use a # before the *T* as:

* #T (carriage return)

The console will then display the two lines of text on the console as:

NOW IS THE TIME FOR ALL GOOD
MEN TO COME TO THE AID OF THEIR
*

Now load the remaining portion of your text from the file to the computer memory by using a # prefix before *A*.

* #A (carriage return)

Again, the pound sign indicates *all*, and with any command acts on the entire text under control of the command. The editor substitutes the number 65535 for the pound sign — the largest number permitted as a prefix. You may not hear the head load this time. CP/M can only read text a sector at a time. This means the remaining line of text may have already been read with the first append command, and was stored in memory by

CP/M, but was not yet seen by the editor which sees records and files—not sectors (see Figure 9).

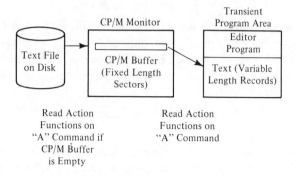

Figure 9. File transfers with the _A_ Command

Now display the entire text as:

```
* # T
NOW IS THE TIME FOR ALL GOOD
MEN TO COME TO THE AID OF THEIR
COUNTRY.
     *
```

If you have a printer, you may type the text to the printer by entering a control/P just before the first carriage return as:

```
* # T (control/P) (carriage return)
```

Be sure the printer is turned on before the carriage return is given. After the text is printed, the printer can be dropped off-line again with another control/P. The control/s command can be used to freeze the printing at any time. The printing will resume if any character is entered from the keyboard.

Now type the command

```
*SMEN(control/Z)WOMEN(carriage return)
```

This will search the entire text for the word _men_, and for the first occurrence of the word will change the word to _women_. Now display the new text as:

```
*B # T
NOW IS THE TIME FOR ALL GOOD
WOMEN TO COME TO THE AID OF THEIR
COUNTRY.
     *
```

Now write two lines of the text to the temporary file with the command:

*2W (carriage return)

Now display the remaining portion of text in the computer memory as:

* #T (carriage return)

The *W* command writes lines of text from the top of the buffer in the computer memory.

Now end your editor session with the command:

*E (carriage return)

This will (1) write the remaining lines of text (both in the computer memory and the input file) to the temporary file, (2) rename the temporary file to TEST.ASC, (3) rename the input file to TEST.BAK, and (4) close both files. Note that the input file is retained just as it was as a back-up with the new name TEST.BAK. The file name TEST.$$$ no longer exists, and a new file with the name TEST.ASC now exists. You can confirm this with the command:

A>DIR TEST.* (carriage return)

EDITOR ERROR MESSAGES

On detecting an error, the editor will print a code to indicate the type of error and the last character read. The codes for error types are as follows:

? Illegal command.

> Memory buffer is full. Use D, K, N, S, or W commands to free up some space.

or

A search or find string of over 100 characters was specified.

Cannot apply the command *n* number of times.

0 Unable to open LIB file in R command.

The editor can recover from any of these without difficulty. Disk errors, however, can generate CP/M error messages and can cause abnormal editor terminations.

THE RUN-AWAY EDITOR

Sometimes there is an error in processing a long file, displaying a lengthy text, or such, and you may wish to stop the editor without leaving the editor or destroying the text. There are two ways to do this.

The first is to type a control/S. The program will continue on typing when you touch any key.

The second is to type a control/Z. This will put you back to the command mode and from this point you can choose your own direction.

EXERCISES

1. List the editor commands by classes and briefly describe each type.
2. If no value is given for n in an nA command, what value for n is assumed by the editor?
3. How does the computer memory size affect the editor's operation?
4. When you used the command $2W$ on the second example, you probably did not hear the disk head load. Why?
5. Which of the following files could not be edited from the editor?

LOAD.COM   EDITOR.COM
FBIOS.ASM   PRINT.HEX
TASK.BAS   LEDGER.ASM

6. What happens when a secondary name is not used with a file to be called with the editor?

CHAPTER 9

Word Processing and Spoolers

Word processing is a fundamental function that almost every computer system should be capable of performing. This is one application program that almost everyone (even without computer training) should be able to use. Preparing programs, letters, and manuscripts all involve word processing. If you hate to write letters, you will have so much fun with a good word processor that you will be swamping the relatives with mail. Authors love word processors and find it increases their productivity so that they can concentrate on the more creative aspects of their writing.

Almost any computer system can be used for word processing and generally not much memory is required. A good printer is necessary. You should use one of the converted selectrics if funds are minimal, or a daisy-wheel (or thimble) printer if you have the funds. Dot-matrix printers are not adequate for word processing. The printer should be capable of printing both upper and lower case characters. You can start with a cassette-based system (we did), but a diskette-based CP/M system will dramatically improve your productivity.

Once the hardware is assembled, you will need to find the software to meet your needs.

EDITORS AND FORMATTERS

Word processing involves two functions:

1. editing
2. formatting

With some software, both of these functions are done by a single program; with other systems, two separate programs are involved.

Editing involves setting up the text. The text is entered, displayed in raw form on the video screen, and any necessary corrections made. A simple editor can search for character strings and change them, merge files, and read paragraphs from stored libraries on a disk. A more complex editor can also move paragraphs around to reform ideas, invert sentences, correct spelling, and permit text to be modified in a wide variety of user-oriented techniques.

A **formatter** does the final printing of the text. It pages the text to the forms or pages you are using, formats material to the correct place on the page, adds titles and page numbers, indents, and centers text where needed. Justification and margin control are also format functions. Normally the formatting is done by embedding character combinations in the text at the beginning of a line. With the TEX formatter, for example, the line

.he THIS IS A TEST

would print the line THIS IS A TEST as a heading on each page that is printed. The period at the beginning of the line tells the formatter the next two characters are a command.

EDITORS

CP/M includes an editor. This editor is usable as a stand alone editor for word processing. Spend some time learning all the command structures and experiment on letters and correspondence.

FORMATTERS

With CP/M, all you need to do fancy word processing is a formatter. Most cost less than $100. This book was processed using a CP/M editor and a text formatter. TEX and a few other formatters function identically, even using the same commands. Avoid the BASIC text formatters. They are entirely too slow in text justifying for most applications.

Figure 10 is an example of raw text created by the CP/M editor with formatting commands embedded in the text. Note that each command is at the beginning of a line and begins with a period. Numbers are used with the command to control the amount of indentation, spacing, or margin. Values not defined by the user are set by default. Figure 11 shows the final text after processing by FORMAT. The raw data file is built with the editor as TEST.TEX. To print the final copy, the command

A>FORMAT TEST PRINTER

is used. Output can also be directed to a disk file or console instead of the printer. The full text processor command structure is shown in Table 2.

COMBINED EDITORS AND FORMATTERS

If you really do a lot of word processing, you should look into purchasing a combined editor/formatter. Two examples are the SELECT™ and Word Star™ word processors. Word Star and SELECT are formattable word processors that compare with the best professional systems, but are expensive (about $500). SELECT is a trademark of Select Information Systems. Word Star is a trademark of Micropro, Inc.

THE SPOOLER

After using your computer for a few months, you may discover much of your time is spent waiting for the printer. The computer is fast, but must wait as the slow printer completes its work. Even when the printer is printing, the computer is really sitting idle most of the time. It would be more productive if you could capture this idle time of the computer while the printer is printing.

A **spooler** does exactly this. Output going to the printer is captured by CP/M and sent to a disk file instead. Then, during the computer idle time, it directs the information in this disk file to the printer. In effect, you can be using the terminal for inputting and editing information while the printer is apparently typing something else.

There are some limitations. The spooler actually modifies the CP/M system in operation, and as such only works with specific systems (as low density, eight inch diskette). The spooler is available from most CP/M software supplirs at a nominal cost.

The spooler works with any program which directs output to the printer. The spooler is turned on or off with simple commands.

.11 70
.po 5
.fo
.ce
APPENDIX F: GLOSSARY
.sp 2
.in 5
.ti 0
addressable cursor—a video cursor that can be moved by software
from the computer.
.sp
.ti 0
APL (A Programming Language)—a high-level programming
language primarily used for list and array processing. Highly
compact source language with special symbols and often requires a
special keyboard and printer.
.sp
.ti 0
application program—a program for a particular use as a word
processor, general ledger, or mailing list processor.
.sp
.ti 0
ASCII (American National Standard Code for Information
Interchange)—a standard code of seven or eight bits used for
information exchange between computer systems.
.sp
.ti 0
ASCII files—data files consisting entirely of ASCII characters, as a
letter file for a word processing program.
.sp
.ti 0
assemble—to translate a program from an assembly language to a
computer machine language.
.sp
.ti 0
assembler—a computer program that converts a program in a
symbolic machine language to an executable form in machine
language. The CP/M assembler converts a source program to a
HEX file form, and requires the LOAD program to convert this to an
executable form.
.sp
.ti 0

assembly-level program—a program in a language in which the instructions are usually one-to-one correspndence with the computer instructions. Such a program is highly specific to a particular type of microprocessor (as 8080 or 6502) and requires extensive modifications to use on another type of system.

Figure 10. Editor input file to Formatter

APPENDIX F: GLOSSARY

addressable cursor—a video cursor that can be moved by software from the computer.

APL (A Programming Language)—a high-level programming language primarily used for list and array processing. Highly compact source language with special symbols and often requires a special keyboard and printer.

application program—a program for a particular use as a word processor, general ledger, or mailing list processor.

ASCII (American National Standard Code for Information Interchange)—a standard code of seven or eight bits used for information exchange between computer systems.

ASCII files—data files consisting entirely of ASCII characters, as a letter file for a word processing program.

assemble—to translate a program from an assembly language to a computer machine language.

assembler—a computer program that converts a program in a symbolic machine language to an executable form in machine language. The CP/M assembler converts a source program to a HEX file form, and requires the LOAD program to convert this to an executable form.

assembly-level program—a program in a language in which the instructions are usually one-to-one correspondence with the computer instructions. Such a program is highly specific to a particular type of microprocessor (as 8080 or 6502) and requires extensive modifications to use on another type of system.

Figure 11. Output of Formatter

AD	right justify turned on
BPn	begin a new page with page number n
BR	stop filling this line and begin a new line
CEn	center the next n lines
DPn	begin a new page if the next n lines will not fit this page
DS	start double-spacing
HExxxxx	define heading for each page
HMn	define number of lines between heading and first line
IG	ignore all lines until the next command is given
INn	indent all lines n spaces
LI	print lines until the next command exactly as given
LLn	sets number of characters per line
LSn	sets vertical spacing between lines to n spaces
MBn	sets number of lines to be left blank at the bottom of the page
MTn	sets number of lines in top margin
NA	turns off adjust, permits TEX to fill short lines
OP	omit page numbers
PAn	ejects n blank pages
PLn	sets page length to n lines
PNn	starts page numbering with page n
POn	sets left margin at n spaces
PPn	inserts one blank line and indents the next line n spaces
QI	quit indenting
SPn	space n lines
SS	sets vertical line spacing to single space
TIn	indents the next line n spaces

Table 2. Format Commands

To start the spooler, type:

A>SPOOL

The computer will then wait for one of three commands:

I Start spooler (initialize)
S Suspend spooler
R Restart spooler

Type the upper case I and the next question is displayed:

ENTER DISK DRIVE (A, B, C, D)

Respond with the drive containing a disk for the spooler files. Choose one with a minimum of activity. The next question will then be displayed:

ENTER NO. OF SPOOL FILES (1-6).

Entering a number now reconfigures CP/M and starts buffering the printer output. SPOOL can be stopped with the command

A>SPOOL S

The specified files will be printed and, when printing is complete, the spooler will automatically stop.

EXERCISES

1. What is an editor?
2. What is a formatter?
3. What is a spooler?
4. How is hardware for a word processing system different from many computer systems?

CHAPTER 10

CP/M Compatible Programming Languages

Programs can be written in a variety of languages. A CP/M program in machine language, ready to load and use, is a COM file. Some utilities are included with CP/M as COM files. Typical COM files included with the CP/M are the DDT, ASM, ED, and DUMP programs. They are ready to load and use. Since they are in the machine's own language, they are difficult to modify but can be studied with a disassembler if you are adventurous.

High level language source files are in a more readable language. Assembler source files are in 8080 mneumonics. BASIC and PASCAL source files are very readable. Almost all programming is done with some type of higher level source language.

High level languages are bridges between the application program being developed or used and the operating system (Figure 12). They permit programmers to develop efficient, complex programs quickly and to modify these programs to meet specific applications with a minimum of cost and time. A given high-level language will permit you to use many application programs on the market. A given application program, however, will run only a specific high-level language, often made only by a specific manufacturer.

HIGH LEVEL LANGUAGES OR
ASSEMBLER LEVEL PROGRAMS

Not all application programs require a high level language. Some are written in **assembly-level language**. Assembly language programs are almost a machine level code. They run faster, use less memory, and generally cost more because of the large amount of development time they require. As a general rule in purchasing word processors, sorters, and data base management programs you should look for the faster assembly-level programs. Financial and statistical programs, mailing list programs, and games should generally be purchased in high-level languages. A word processor written in BASIC, for example, will probably require too much time to justify a text file with many lines (Table 3).

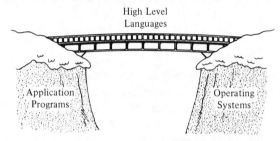

Figure 12. High level languages are bridges

ASSEMBLER PROGRAMS	BASIC PROGRAMS
1. Long development time	Short development time
2. Large development cost	Small development cost
3. Difficult to modify	Easy to modify
4. Fast in running	Slow in running
5. Use less memory	Use considerable memory
6. Difficult to get source from program	Easy to get source in most cases

Table 3. Comparison of Assembler Program vs. BASIC

In shopping for high-level languages to use with your CP/M you will certainly encounter plenty of confusion, questions, and issues. The most important questions depend, however, on whether you plan to purchase programs or develop your own programs.

If you plan to purchase your application programs, what language will these application programs be using? The application program determines which high-level language you pur-chase — not vice versa. In some cases you may wish to purchase several high-level languages to give you a broader market base from which to choose your application programs.

If you plan to develop your own programs or have a consul-tant write your programs for you, the most important con-siderations are ease of use and debugging (which translates to development time and money), learning speed and familiarity, and features.

The cost of any high-level language is only a small part of your total system cost, perhaps 5% at the most. A cheaper package generally doesn't save you too much money in the long run. Quality and ease of use are more important.

There are no generally accepted standards for many high-level languages, particularly BASIC. A program written in Microsoft BASIC may not run with CBASIC and vice-versa. High-level languages now on the market include BASIC (several versions), FORTRAN, COBOL, PASCAL, Tiny-C, and APL. We will talk more about these later. There are few standards, and a given BASIC program will work with only a particular BASIC compiler or interpreter. In some cases the change may not in-volve much time (or cost), but in other cases it could be expen-sive. You may want to purchase several compilers and inter-preters to give you access to a wider application software market and reduce your own software development expense for your own application programs (Figure 13).

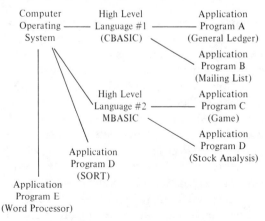

Figure 13. Application programs and high level languages work together

INTERPRETER, COMPILER, OR PROCESSOR?

Some high-level languages are referred to as compilers, others as interpreters. Often the same language (as Microsoft BASIC) can be purchased either as a compiler or interpreter. Which should you buy?

A **compiler** (see Figure 14) is run once with the application program and converts the program to a machine-level language. The program is then run as a machine-level language as many times as desired. Because the program is always run in machine-level language, it runs rapidly and efficiently using the resources of the computer to its maximum advantage. An example would be the Microsoft FORTRAN. The final program is a COM file, and looks and behaves just like any program written in assembly language.

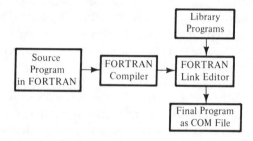

Figure 14. The FORTRAN compiler

An **interpreter** is different from a compiler in that the application program itself is in the computer memory with the interpreter. The program is read by the interpreter and executed on a statement-by-statement basis. It can be stopped or restarted at any point, with variables examined at that point. Debugging is easy, but programs tend to run slowly. An example would be the Microsoft BASIC interpreter. The interpreter is easier to use in software development than a compiler, but it uses more memory and the final program always runs slowly (Table 4).

Some high-level languages are in a never-never land somewhere between pure interpreters and compilers. Two popular examples are CBASIC and Pascal. CBASIC is called a compiler, but acts, in some ways, like an interpreter. The source language is converted to a run-time code by a compile process,

INTERPRETER	COMPILER
Debugging is easy and fast. Programs can be stopped anywhere at any time and variables examined, often altered.	Difficult to debut programs — programs must be run through the compiler after each fix. Problem tracing can be difficult.
Memory intensive. The interpreter must reside in core with the program.	Very memory efficient. No space is used by the high-level language a run-time.
Considered to be easier to develop and therefore less expensive.	Generally more expensive to develop and debug than an interpreter.
Runs slowly, as program is interpreted at run time.	Runs fast, as run-time program is written in a near machine-level language.
Source code of application program is available to user and difficult to protect.	Source code of application program is not available to user and is protected.

Table 4. The Computer vs. the Interpreter

but the final code is not machine level. It must still be interpreted by a run-time monitor that is slow and memory intensive. Some versions of Pascal on CP/M machines are similar. The source is converted to a P-code that must be interpreted at run-time by an interpreter that is also in the computer memory.

A **preprocessor** is a high-level language that can compile a source code in a specific form to a code that can be read by another compiler. This expands the capabilities of the compiler at the overhead of an additional compile (see Figure 15). An example would be RATFOR (see software appendix). An extremely powerful word processor can be written a RATFOR program and compiled a FORTRAN program. The FORTRAN, in turn, is compiled to a very fast and efficient machine-level language program. If a user needs specific modifications, the programmer goes back to the RATFOR source, implements them, and then compiles the source again. The original source is always kept by the programmer and changes are made at low development costs. The final output is as efficient and fast as any product on the market and protected (the source code is not sold).

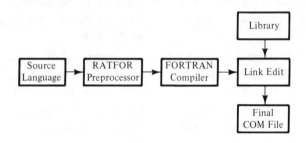

Figure 15. The RATFOR preprocessor

AN OVERVIEW OF SOME HIGH LEVEL LANGUAGES

The following sections discuss some of the more popular currently available higher level languages. Appendix C lists the suppliers' full names and addresses.

Microsoft BASIC

This was the earliest high-level language available to microcomputer users. Even its earliest versions are surprisingly clean, have few errors, and are quite powerful with many extended features. The first version for CP/M (4.1) has a problem in processing random files of over 16,384 bytes in size. Later versions have fixed this problem. This BASIC has more acceptance and a wider user base than probably any high-level language. Versions with almost identical features are available for other operating systems as the Radio Shack TRS-80 and Heathkit computers. This means you will have plenty of application programs from which to choose. Both compiler and interpreter versions are now available for CP/M.

An editing feature is built into Microsoft BASIC, and programs can be edited without leaving the interpreter. Programs can also be saved in ASCII mode and edited with the CP/M editor. A program entered under the editor can also be read by Microsoft BASIC.

In these BASIC interpreters the input source code is immediately converted to a condensed form to minimize space and increase speed. This BASIC is also probably the fastest micro-computer BASIC on the market for most applications. Using the interpreter version, you will find programs are fast to write, fast to debug, and your learning time is short.

Early versions of Microsoft BASIC (version 4.5) permitted random files with records of only a 128 byte length. This is a disadvantage with some software using key-oriented files and data base management software. The last versions of Microsoft BASIC now permit random files with records of any length.

The new Microsoft BASIC version 5.0 now includes protection features on programs written to disk. A protected program cannot be listed or edited. As a result I expect more business application software using MBASIC will soon be available.

Microsoft BASIC is fairly expensive ($300), but it is a proven product with a wide user base that includes far more than CP/M-based systems.

CBASIC2

This is the third generation of the earliest BASIC available on CP/M machines. Originally written by Gordon Eubanks, CBASIC2 is now marketed and supported by Digital Research, Inc.

CBASIC2 is often marketed as a compiler, but is in reality neither a compiler nor an interpreter. CBASIC2 converts the BASIC source code to a special intermediate language, and this intermediate language file is run as often as desired by calling it with CRUN2. For example:

```
A>CBAS2 STARTREK
```

creates an intermediate language file STARTREK.INT from STARTREK.BAS. This INT file can then be executed by entering:

```
A>CRUN2 STARTREK
```

CBASIC2 uses binary floating point calculations, rounding off calculated values. Microsoft BASIC, in contrast, uses binary-coded decimal arithmetic and truncates beyond its specified precision. Although CBASIC2 is often used for commercial applications for this reason, Microsoft BASIC has plenty of precision to obtain the necessary accuracy for almost any application. Another feature of CBASIC, which is valuable to software

	CBASIC	CBASIC2	BASIC-80 4.1	BASIC-80 5.0	TARBELL BASIC
long variable names	yes	yes	no	yes	yes
multi-line functions	no	yes	no	no	no
random files	yes	yes	yes	yes	yes
random file records any length	yes	yes	no	yes	yes
source language available	no	no	no	no	yes
program chaining	no	yes	no	yes	no
cost	$100	$120		$325	$148
compiler or interpreter	comp	comp	int	either	int
matrix operators	no	no	no	no	no
error trapping	no	no	yes	yes	no
multi-dimensional arrays	yes	yes	yes	yes	yes
match function	yes	yes	yes	yes	yes
formatted print statement	yes	yes	yes	yes	yes
random # generator	yes	yes	*	yes	yes
PEEK/POKE	yes	yes	yes	yes	yes
user subroutines permitted	yes	yes	yes	yes	yes
non-numeric labels	no	no	no	no	yes
LINPUT	yes	yes	yes	yes	yes
line printer output	yes	yes	yes	yes	yes
error codes	codes	codes	full ASCII	full ASCII	abbreviated
command data	no	yes	no	yes	no
while/wend	yes	yes	no	yes	no
dynamic string space	yes	yes	no	yes	yes

* Generated series is always identical.

Table 5. BASIC Comparison Chart

developers, is the coded nature of the INT file. A company can sell the INT file without the source and protect the source code.

CBASIC2 programs are more difficult to debug because of the extra steps necessary to build the INT file each time the program is changed, but a good programmer shouldn't have any bugs in their program anyway—right?

If you need the extra speed, CBASIC is also sold in a compiler form as CB-80. Using CB-80, a program in CBASIC code can be compiled to a machine language COM file, and in this way gain the speed of assembly level programming.

Pascal

Pascal is touted by its users as the language of the future. It is designed to permit structured programming. The programmer organizes his program in blocks, defining each block and then writing each as an independent *module*. A program written this way has fewer errors from the start and is easier to modify, debug, and change. In an educational environment many people find Pascal is easier to learn than BASIC.

Pascal has string processing limitations and needs features added to be competitive with other high-level languages. Like BASIC, it is non-standard and most manufacturers have their own version. Application program choice is small at the present time, but should grow rapidly. It is excellent for applications such as electronic conferencing systems or operating system development.

With CP/M systems, some of the Pascal compilers convert the source code to a P-code language, and this run-time module is run with a P-code interpreter (similar to CBASIC). This run-time interpreter uses memory space. In addition, interpreted programs will run slowly against a program written in a machine language (as the output of FORTRAN program).

Pascal really shines in non-CP/M systems designed to interpret P-codes directly as a machine language—as the Pascal Microengine. In this case the interpreter is not needed. The Pascal Microengine, however, is not a CP/M system.

Tarbell BASIC

The youngest BASIC on the market is designed to offer a lot of features for only $100. You will find this BASIC has almost all the features of its expensive competitors at very little cost. Many manufacturers of high-level languages will not sell you their source coding, but you will get the source code for the Tarbell BASIC I/O with your order (you configure it for your system), and the remainder of the source code will only cost you $25. The source can be reconfigured easily for non-CP/M systems using CP/M file structures, and with the source code you could add your own interesting features (as, for example, ISAM file structures). The Tarbell BASIC is slower than other BASICs, but the price is low.

FORTRAN

FORTRAN has developed as one of the finest and most widely used high-level languages. It is primarily designed for scientific applications, but many other types of programs can be written. FORTRAN has no string processing capability, but this can be added with subroutines or with the use of a preprocessor such as RATFOR. The Microsoft FORTRAN is quite powerful with almost all standard features included. The final output is a fast and efficient machine level program.

Using KISS, a user can extend the FORTRAN for keyword access of a data base system (see below).

APL

APL has great capability in processing string arrays and character manipulation. The language is also very efficient, and several lines of BASIC or FORTRAN can be coded to a single statement in APL. Special symbols are used, and most printers and keyboards will not have these symbols.

RATFOR

RATFOR is an extremely powerful preprocessor for FOR-TRAN. Used with Microsoft FORTRAN, you will find it probably one of the best development tools on the market for applications involving sequential files, as word processing and mailing lists. With a little effort, RATFOR can also be used for random files and data base management.

KBASIC

KBASIC is the Microsoft BASIC version 4.5 with extended functions for keyword access of data base files. Data base file management is discussed in Volume II, but KBASIC was our choice for quick programs we wrote for mailing list processing, diskette file management, and information retrieval. In these applications the user must access information quickly against keywords or descriptors. A similar version of this data base managemnt system is also sold as KISS to use with Microsoft FORTRAN.

EXERCISES

1. Name six high level languages.
2. What is a compiler?
3. What is an interpreter?
4. What are the primary advantages and disadvantages of using BASIC against assembly-level programming?
5. What are the pros and cons using a high-level compiler versus an assembler?

APPENDIX A

CP/M Memory Map

```
        ┌─┐ ┌──────────────────────────┐
        │ │ │         BIOS*            │
        │ │ │       (512 Bytes)        │
        │ │ ├──────────────────────────┤
  FDOS ─┤ │ │                          │
        │ │ │         BDOS             │
        │ │ │       (3328 Bytes)       │
        └─┘ ├──────────────────────────┤
            │         CCP              │
            │       (2048 Bytes)       │
            ├──────────────────────────┤
            │                          │
            │                          │
            │                          │
            │       Transient          │
            │       Program            │
            │        Area              │
            │                          │
            │                          │
            │                          │
            │                          │
            ├──────────────────────────┤
            │        256 Bytes         │
            │    (Reserved for CP/M)   │
            └──────────────────────────┘
```

*Actual size of BIOS segment
will vary between CP/M versions.

How to Get Started with CP/M

FIRST PAGE MEMORY MAP

Location (Hex)

0-2	Jump to warm start entry in BIOS
3	Iobyte, if used
4	Default drive number
5-7	Jump to low end of BDOS (defines end of TPA if CCP is overlayed)
8-37	Reserved for user interrupt control
38-3A	Jump used by DDT in breakpoint mode
3B-5B	Not currently used
5C-7C	File information for files loaded to transient program area
7D-7F	Not used
80-FF	Disk buffer (128 bytes)

CP/M DISK MAP (IBM FORMAT)

Track #	Sector #	CP/M Module
00	01	Cold Start Loader
01	01-17	BDOS
01	18-26	BIOS (all of this track is not used)
02	01-26	Directory
03-76		Files, Data

CP/M BUILT-IN COMMANDS AND UTILITIES

Built-in Commands

ERA	erase specified file(s)
DIR	list directory
REN	rename specified file
SAVE	save transient program area
TYPE	display a file

CP/M Programs

STAT	list directory and disk storage information
ASM	assemble a source file
LOAD	create a COM file from a HEX file

DDT	debugs CP/M programs
PIP	copies files
ED	edits and creates files
SYSGEN	creates a new CP/M system
SUBMIT	batch processes CP/M programs
DUMP	displays a CP/M program
CPM (or MOVCPM)	used in modifying a CP/M system

CP/M CONTROL CODE LISTING

Rubout	Delete and echo last character typed
Control/U	Delete the entire console line
Control/X	Delete the entire console line
Control/R	Display current command line
Control/E	Local carriage return – no command issued
Control/C	Create a warm boot (BIOS is not reloaded)
Control/Z	(Special to editor and PIP)
Control/P	Copy all console output to printer
Control/S	Freeze console temporarily

CP/M EDITOR COMMAND SUMMARY

nA	append *n* lines from disk file
+B	set character pointer to start or end of buffer
nC	move character pointer *n* positions
nD	delete *n* characters
E	close and end edit
nF	find *n*th occurrence (memory buffer only)
H	close and re-open files
I	insert characters
nJ	juxtaposition strings
nK	kill *n* lines
nL	move character pointer *n* lines
nM	execute macro *n* times
nN	find (entire file) *n*th occurrence of string
O	return to original file
nP	display next 20 lines *n* times
Q	quit with no file changes
R	read library or stored lines from disk
nS	change string
nT	type or display *n* lines
U	lower case to upper case switch
V	switch to line number mode

nW   write *n* lines to output file
nX   store *n* lines in disk file

CP/M PIP COMMAND SUMMARY

B   block mode transfer
Dn   terminate at *n* columns
E   echo transfer to console
F   remove form feeds from file
H   hex check on transfer
I   Ignore :00 records in transfer
L   translate upper case to lower
N   add line numbers
O   object file transfer
Pn   include page ejects at every *n* lines
Qs↑z   quit copying when string *s* is found
Ss↑z   start copying when string *s* is found
Tn   expand tabs to *n* spaces
U   translate lower case to upper
V   verify transfer
Z   zero parity bits

(The ↑ key indicates to hold the control key down while pressing the next key.)

APPENDIX B

CP/M Hardware Suppliers

The following directory is a list of CP/M hardware manufacturers and OEM suppliers.

The author and publisher make no warranty as to the quality, availability, or applicability of the listed hardware for the user's specific needs.

This listing is updated periodically in subsequent book printings. Companies wishing to update their listing or add a listing should send information to Carl Townsend, CP/M Hardware Directory, dilithium Press, 11000 S.W. 11th Street, Suite E, Beaverton, OR 97005.

ABCS (Advanced Business Computer Systems) Intl. Inc.
426 W. 2nd Street
Davenport, IA 52801
(319) 323-7857

ADES (Adaptive Data & Energy Systems)
2627 Pomona Blvd.
Pomona, CA 91768
(714) 594-5858

Algorithmics Inc.
177 Worcester Road
Wellesley, MA 02181
(617) 237-7226

Adtek System Science Co. Ltd.
16-9, Minamisengen,
Nishi-ku
Yokohama-shi
Japan

Alspa Computer
5215 Scotts Valley Drive
Scotts Valley, CA 95066
(408) 438-3326

Altos Computer Systems
2360 Bering Drive
San Jose, CA 95131
(408) 946-6700

AOS
PO Box 26027
4801 Indian School Rd. NE
Albuquerque, NM 87125
(505) 265-3511

Applied Technology
PO Box 3042
Tucson, AZ 85702
(602) 795-9929

Archives Inc.
404 West 35th Street
Davenport, IA 52806
(319) 386-7401 (in Iowa)
(319) 386-7280
(800) 553-6950

Artelonics Corp.
Subsidiary of
Shell Canada Ltd.
2952 Bunker Hill Lane
Santa Clara, CA 95050
(408) 727-3071

Astrocom Corporation
120 West Plato Blvd.
St. Paul, MN 55107
(612) 227-8651

Aurelec
Prayogashala-Auroville
Kottakuppam, Tamilnadu
India 605104

Austin Microcomputers
3415 Greystone, Suite 302
Austin, TX 78731
(512) 443-3508

**Automation
Statham Pty. Ltd.**
47 Birch Street
Bankstown, NSW 2200
Australia
02-709-4144

AVL Incorporated
500 Hillside Avenue
Atlantic Highlands,
NJ 07716
(201) 291-4400

FW Backus
3239 El Camino Real
Palo Alto, CA 94306
(415) 493-4343

**BMC Computer
Corporation**
860 East Walnut Street
Carson, CA 90746
(213) 323-2600

BMG Microsystems Ltd.
Microhouse, Hawksworth
Swindon, Wiltshire
England SN2 1D2
(793) 37813

Beam Business Center
Centurian House
129 Deans Gate
Manchester, M33 WA1
England

Bobst Graphic
165 University Ave.
Suite 105
Palo Alto, CA 94301
(415) 326-3885

California Computer Systems
250 Caribbean Drive
Sunnyvale, CA 94086
(408) 734-5811

Callan Data Systems
2637 Townsgate Road
Westlake Village, CA 91361
(805) 497-6837
(408) 738-8450 (sales office)

Cambridge Telecommunications
20 Blanchard
Burlington, MA 01902
(617) 273-5930

Campbell Scientific
PO Box 551
Logan, UT 84321
(801) 753-2342

CASU Electronics
17 Stonefield Close
Victoria Park Industrial Estate
South Ruislip
England

Centa Systems, Inc.
1613 S. River Dr.
Tempe, AZ 85281
(602) 967-1421 x. 234

Chromatics
Park Lucerne Executive Center
790 Lucerne Drive, #15A
Sunnyvale, CA 94086
(408) 730-1023
1-800-241-9467
(GA Corp. Office)

CM Technologies Inc.
525 University Ave.
Palo Alto, CA 94301
(415) 326-9150

Columbia Data Products
8990, Route 108
Columbia, MD 21045
(301) 992-3400

Comark
257 Crescent Street
Waltham, MA 02154
(617) 894-7000

Commercial Computer, Inc.
7884 12th Ave. South
Minneapolis, MN 55420
(612) 854-2309

COMPAL, Inc.
6300 Variel Ave.
Woodland Hills, CA 91367

Computer Mart of New Jersey
501 Route 27
Iselin, NJ 08830
(201) 283-0600

Computer Center
9, De-La-Beche
Swansea SA 3EX
England

Computer Marketing Corporation
CMC International Division
11058 Main, Suite 1125
Bellevue, WA 98004
(206) 453-9777

Computer Methods
Box 709
Chatsworth, CA 91311
(213) 994-7763

Computer Systems Design
906 North Main
Wichita, KN 67203
(316) 265-1120

Computer Technology
6311 Federal Blvd.
Denver, CO 80221
(303) 427-4438

COSMOS
Astar Intl. Inc.
5676 Francis Ave.
Chino, CA 91710
(714) 627-9887

CROMEMCO
280 Bernardo Ave.
Mountain View, CA 94043
(415) 964-7400

Crystal Electronics
40 Magdalene Road
Torquay, Devon
England
080322699

Daisy Systems
Nieuweweg 279
6600 AC WWijchen
Netherlands

Datadisk Systems
PO Box 195
Poway, CA 92064
(714) 578-3831

Datamac Computer Systems
680 Almanor Ave.
Sunnyvale, CA 94086
(408) 735-0323

Dataspeed, Inc.
1302 Noe St.
San Francisco, CA 94044

Delta Products
15392 Assembly Lane
Huntington Beach,
CA 92649
(714) 898-1492

Devasoft
Postfach 34.7222
FL 9490
Vaduz
Liechtenstein

Digi-Log
Babylon Road
Horsham, PA 19044
(215) 672-0800

Digilog Business Systems
PO Box 355
Montgomeryville, PA 18936

**Digital Equipment Corp.
(DEC)**
Terminals Product Group
MR2-2/M67, One Iron Way
Marlborough, MA 01752
1-800-258-1577
(603) 884-7492 (in NH)
1-800-267-5250 (in Canada)
011-41-22-93-33-11
(in Europe)

Digital Microsystems
1840 Embarcadero
Oakland, CA 94606
(415) 582-3686

Distributed Computer Systems
223 Crescent Street
Waltham, MA 02154

DIT-MCO Intl.
5612 Brighton Terrace
Kansas City, MO 64130
(816) 444-9700

Durango Systems
3003 North First Street
San Jose, CA 95134
(408) 946-5000

Dynabyte
521 Cottonwood Drive
Milpitas, CA 95035
(408) 263-1221

Dynasty Computer Corp.
14240 Midway Rd.
Dallas, TX 75234
(214) 386-8634

E & U Engel Consulting
1719 S. Carmelina Ave.
Los Angeles, CA 90025
(213) 820-4231

Eidos Systems Corp.
1200 Beechwood Ave.
Nashville, TN 37217
(615) 385-0730

Elbit Computers, Ltd.
PO Box 5390
Haifa
Israel
31050

Electro Analytic Systems
PO Box 102
Ledgewood, NJ 07852
(201) 584-4554

Electronic Control Systems
7A Gibbes St.
Charswood, Sydney
NSW
Australia
4065711

Equinox Computer Systems
16 Anning St.
New Inn Yard
London EC2A 3HB
England
01-739 2387/9

Evolution Computer Systems Corp.
250 East Emerson Ave.
Orange, CA 92665
(714) 974-7670
(800) 432-7257, x821
(outside CA)

Exidy Systems
1234 Elko Drive
Sunnyvale, CA 94086
(408) 734-9831

Exo Electronics Company
1089 Airport Road
Minden, NV 89423
(702) 782-8166

Fet/Test
160 Albright Way, Suite E
Los Gatos, CA 95030
(408) 374-3613

Findex
20775 South Western Ave.
Torrance, CA 90501
(213) 533-6842

Fischer-Freitas
2175 Adams Ave.
San Leandro, CA 94577
(415) 635-7615

FMG/Applied Data Corp.
Box 16020
Ft. Worth, TX 76133
(817) 294-2510

Frontrunner Computer Ind.
160 A East Plumb Lane
Reno, NV 89502
(702) 358-1100

G & G Engineering
13708 Doolittle Drive
San Leandro, CA 94577
(415) 895-0798

Galaxy Computers Inc.
570 E. El Camino Real,
Suite B
Sunnyvale CA 94087
(408) 737-7000

Gnat Computers, Inc.
7895 Convoy Court, Bldg. 6
San Diego, CA 92111
(714) 560-0433

Godbout Electronics
Building 725
Oakland Airport, CA 94614
(415) 562-0630

Heath Company
521 Cottonwood Drive
Benton Harbor, MI 49022
(616) 982-3210

Heurikon Corp.
3001 Latham Drive
Madison, WI 53713
(608) 271-8700

Hewlett Packard
3000 Hanover
Palo Alto, CA 94304
(408) 725-8111

Hindustan Computers, Ltd.
505 Siddharth
96 Nehru Place
New Delhi, 110019
India

**IBC/Integrated Business
Computers**
21592 Marilla Street
Chatsworth, CA 91311
(213) 882-9007

**IBM Information Systems
Division**
PO Box 1328
Boca Raton, FL 33432

Ideas, Inc.
10759 Tucker Street
Beltsville, MD 20705
(301) 937-3600

IMS International
Corporate Offices
2800 Lockheed Way
Carson City, NV 89701
(702) 883-7611

Industrial Micro Systems
628 N. Eckhoff Street
Orange, CA 92688
(714) 978-6966

Info 2000 Corp.
PO Box 945
Los Alamitos, CA 90742
(213) 532-1702

Information Dialogues
2021 Hennepin Avenue
Suite 115
Minneapolis, MN 55413
(612) 331-9210

**Integrated Business
Computers**
22010 S. Wilmington Ave.
Suite 306
Carson, CA 90745
(213) 518-4245

Intelligent Terminal Corp.
2320 SW Freeway
Houston, TX 77098
(713) 529-6696

International Micro Systems
8425 Quivera Road
Lenexa, KA 66215
(913) 888-8330

Intersil Systems Division
1275 Hammerwood Ave.
Sunnyvale, CA 94086
(408) 743-4300

Intertec Data Systems
2300 Broad River Road
Columbia, SC 29210
(803) 798-9100

**ISM (Information Systems
Marketing)**
5161 River Road, Bldg. 20
Bethesda, MD 20016
(301) 986-0773

Ithaca Intersystems, Inc.
1650 Hanshaw Road
Ithaca, NY 14850
(607) 257-0190

Jade Computer Products
4901 West Rosecrans
Hawthorne, CA 90250
(213) 973-7707

Johnson-Laird, Inc.
1556 SW 66th Ave.
Portland, OR 97225
(503) 292-6330

**Kokusai Data Machine
Systems**
276 Nozaki Mitaka
Tokyo 181
Japan
0422-32-4111

Kontron Electronics
630 Price Ave.
Redwood City, CA 94063
(415) 361-1012

**Lanier Business
Products, Inc.**
1700 Chantilly Dr. NE
Atlanta, GA 30324
(800) 241-1706
(404) 321-1244 (collect in GA)

LHA Computers
47 Bedford Street SE
Minneapolis, MN 55414
(612) 378-3721

**Leading Edge
Products, Inc.**
Office Products Division
225 Turnpike Street
Canton, MA 02021
(617) 828-8150
(collect in MA)
1-800-343-6862

Leapac Services
8245 Mediteranean Way
Sacramento, CA 95826
(916) 381-1717

Lexor Corporation
7100 Hayvenhurst Ave.
Van Nuys, CA 91406
(213) 786-1600

Logitek (Interface Software)
Portland Street
Chorley, Lancashire
England PR7 1SF
Chorley 66803

LSI Computers
West House, Stawell
Bridgewater, Somerset
England TA7 9AA
0278-722073

Magnavox
1313 Production Road
Fort Wayne, IN 46808
(219) 482-4411

Magnolia Microsystems
2812 Thorndyke Ave. West
Seattle, WA 98199
(206) 285-7266

**Management Computer
Systems**
1888 Century Park East
Suite 212
Los Angeles, CA 90067
(213) 552-0755

Marfam Corp.
5340 Thornwood Drive
San Jose, CA 95123
(408) 578-3160

Matrox Electronic Systems
5800 Andover Street
Montreal, Quebec H4T 1H4
Canada
(514) 735-1182

**Measurement Systems and
Controls**
1601 Orangewood
Orange, CA 92668
(714) 639-4812

**Micro Applications &
Hardware**
73 Cazneau Ave.
Sausalito, CA 94965
(415) 332-4443

Microbar Systems Inc.
1120 San Antonio Road
Palo Alto, CA 94303
(415) 964-2862

Micro Business Associates
500 Second Street
San Francisco, CA 94107
(415) 957-9195

Microbyte
1198 East Willow Street
Signal Hill
Long Beach, CA 90806
(213) 595-8571

**Microcomputer
Products Intl.**
8-11 Cambridge House
Cambridge Road
Barking, Essex
1G11 8NT
England
01-553-1001

MicroDaSys
PO Box 36051
Los Angeles, CA 90036
(213) 731-0876

Micro-Link Corporation
624 S. Range Line Road
Carmel, IN 46032
(312) 846-1721
(312) 846-1828

Micromation
1620 Montgomery Street
San Francisco, CA 94111
(415) 398-0289

Micronix Systems Inc.
PO Box 401245
Garland, TX 75042
(214) 271-3538

Micropolis
21329 Nordhoff St.
Chatsworth, Ca 91311
(213) 709-3300

Microsoft
400 108th Ave. NE
Suite 200
Bellevue, WA 98004

Micro/Sys Inc.
1353 Foothill Blvd.
La Canada, CA 91011
(213) 790-7957

Micro/Tel
2252 Welsch Industrial Ct.
St. Louis, MO 63141

Micro V Corporation
17791 Skypark Circle
Irvine, CA 92714
(714) 957-1517

Millennium Systems Inc.
19050 Pruneridge Ave.
Cupertino, CA 95014
(408) 996-9109

Modular Systems Corp.
21 Chapel Lane, Yeadon
Leeds, Yorkshire
England LS19 7NX
Leeds 505719

Monolithic Systems Corp.
84 Inverness Circle East
Englewood, CO 80112
(303) 770-7400

Morrow Designs
(Thinker Toys)
5221 Central Ave.
Richmond, CA 94804
(415) 524-2101

MuSYS Corporation
1451 Irvine Blvd.
Suite 11
Tustin, CA 92680
(714) 730-5692

National Multiplex Corp.
260 Lackland Drive
Middlesex, NJ 08846
(701) 356-9200

NEC America, Inc.
1401 Estes Avenue
Elk Grove Village, IL 60007
(312) 228-5900

Neptune UES
7070 Commerce Circle
Pleasanton, CA 94566
(415) 462-1543

NNC Electronics
15631 Computer Lane
Huntington Beach,
CA 92609
(714) 895-8000

Northern Microcomputer
749 River Ave.
Eugene, OR 97404
(503) 688-6771

Northstar Computers Inc.
1440 Fourth Street
Berkeley, CA 94710
(415) 527-6950
(415) 357-8500

Novell Data Systems Inc.
1170 No. Industrial Pk. Dr.
Orem, UT 84057
(800) 453-1188
(801) 226-8202

Ohio Scientific
1333 South Chillicothe Rd.
Aurora, OH 44202
(216) 831-5600

Onyx Systems Inc.
73 East Trimble Road
San Jose, CA 95131
(408) 946-6330

G.M. O'Reilly & Associates
A1
6 Ryde Road
Hunters Hill
North Sydney NSW 2110
Australia
(02) 436-1666

**Osborne Computer
Corporation**
26500 Corporate Ave.
Hayward, CA 94545
(415) 887-8080

Pacific Western Systems
505 East Evelyn
Mt. View, CA 94041
(415) 961-8855

Parasitic Engineering
1101 Ninth Avenue
Oakland, CA 94606
(415) 839-2636

Pentel Corporation
2715 Columbia W.
Torrance, CA 90503
(213) 320-3831

Performance Business Machines
750 Adrian Way
San Rafael, CA 94903
(415) 499-1655

Piiceon, Inc.
Intelligent Systems Div.
2350 Bering Drive
San Jose, CA 95131
(408) 946-8030

Pragmatic Designs Inc.
950 Benicia Avenue
Sunnyvale, CA 94086
(415) 736-8670

Precision Computer Systems
1737 North First Street
Suite 580
San Jose, CA 95112
(408) 279-8228

Prodigy Systems Inc.
497 Lincoln Highway
Iselin, NJ 08830
(201) 283-2000

Q1 Corporation
125 Ricefield Lane
Hauppauge, NY 11787
(516) 543-7800

Quasar Data Products
10330 Brecksville Road
Brecksville, OH 44141
(216) 526-0838

Quay Corporation
PO Box 386
Freehold, NJ 07728
(201) 681-8700

R2E of America
2912 Anthony Lane
Minneapolis, MN 55418
(612) 788-9423

Rair Ltd.
30-32 Neal Street
London WC2H 9PS
England

Rair Microcomputer Corp.
4101 Burton Drive
Santa Clara, CA 95050
(408) 988-1790

Real Time Computer System
28-32 Mill Street
Crewe
England
(0270) 56142

Rennaisance Technology
3347 Vincent Road
Pleasant Hill, CA 94523
(415) 930-7707

John F. Rose Computer Services
33-35 Atchison Street
St. Leonards, NSW 2065
Australia

Rosemount, Inc.
12001 West 78th Street
Eden Prairie, MN 55343
(612) 941-5560 Ext. 352

Rothenberg Information Systems
260 Sheridan Ave.
Palo Alto, CA 94306
(415) 324-8850

Scott Enterprises
627 Orangewood
Newberry Park, CA 91320
(805) 498-1862

SD Systems
PO Box 28810
Dallas, TX 75228

Sierra National Corporation
5037 Ruffner Street
San Diego, CA 92111
(714) 277-4810

Software Source
PO Box 364
Edgecliff NSW 2027
Australia

Symbiotic Systems Inc.
118 Naglee Avenue
Santa Cruz, CA 95060
(408) 425-5533

Systel Computers, Inc.
20370 Town Center Lane
Cupertino, CA 95014
(408) 253-0992

Systems Group
1601 Orangewood
Orange, CA 92668
(714) 633-4460

Tandberg A/S
PO Box 55
Bogerud
Oslo 6
Norway

Tarbell Electronics
950 Dovlen Place, Suite B
Carson, CA 90746
(213) 538-4251

Technology Group, Inc.
860 E. Walnut Street
Carson, CA 90746
(213) 323-2600

TEI
5075 S. Loop East
Houston, TX 77033
(713) 738-2300

Telecomputing Ltd.
Seacourt Tower, West Way
Oxford
England
Oxford 723621

Teletek Enterprises, Inc.
9767 F Business Park Drive
Sacramento, CA 95827
(916) 361-1777

Televideo Systems Inc.
1170 Morse Ave.
Sunnyvale, CA 94086
(408) 745-7760 (in CA)
(800) 538-8725 (outside CA)

Toshiba America, Inc.
Information Processing
Systems Division
2441 Michelle Drive
Tustin, CA 92680
(714) 730-5000

Total Computing
2712 E. Second Street
Newberg, OR 97132
(503) 538-2185

Transam Components Ltd.
59-61 Theobalds' Road
London
England WC1

United Technologies
50 Galaxy Blvd.
Unit #8
Toronto, Ontario
Canada M9W 4Y5
(416) 675-1590

Vector Graphic, Inc.
31364 Via Colinas
Westlake Village, CA 91361
(800) 382-3367 (in CA)
(800) 423-5857

Vector International
Research Park
B-3030 Leuven
Belgium

Vista Computer Company
1317 E. Edinger Ave.
Santa Ana, CA 92705
(714) 953-0523

Wang Laboratories Inc.
One Industrial Ave.
Lowell, MA 01851
(617) 459-5000

White Computer Company
1876 Industrial Way
Redwood City, CA 94063
(415) 364-7570

Xerox Corp.
Office Products Div.
1341 Mockingbird Lane
Dallas, TX 75247
(213) 536-9129

Xitex
9861 Chartwell Drive
Dallas, TX 75243
(214) 349-2490

Xycom
750 North Maple Road
Saline, MI 48176
(313) 429-4971

Zendex Corporation
6680 Sierra Lane
Dublin, CA 94566
(415) 829-1284

Zenith Data Systems
1000 Milwaukee Ave.
Glenview, IL 60025
(312) 391-8860

Zentec
2400 Walsh Ave.
Santa Clara, CA 95050
(408) 727-7662

Zobex
7343-J Ronson Road
San Diego, CA 92111
(714) 571-6971

APPENDIX C

CP/M Software Suppliers

The following software directory is a listing of CP/M compatible software. There are three listings:

1. Software alphabetically by name.
2. Software alphabetically by category.
3. Vendor list.

The author and publisher make no warranty as to the quality of the listed software or the applicability of any software for the user's specific needs.

This listing is updated periodically in subsequent book printings. Companies wishing to update their listing or add a listing should address information to Carl Townsend, CP/M Software Directory, dilithium Press, 11000 S.W. 11th Street, Suite E, Beaverton, OR 97005.

The following is the format for the alphabetical listing:

> Software Title
> Class/Application
> (Memory Size Required) Price*
> Primary Vendor

*Some software titles are trademarks of the vending company. If this is true, the price line of the listing will contain an asterisk.

In some cases, memory size and cost were not available.

CP/M SOFTWARE LISTED ALPHABETICALLY

ABSTAT
Research/Statistics
$400.00
Anderson-Bell Company

ACCESS/80
Development/RPG
(48K) $295.00
Friends Software

ACCOUNTING PLUS
Business/Accounting
Systems Plus

ACT I
Development/
Macro Assembler
(24K) $125.00   *
Digital Marketing

ACT II
Development/
Macro Assembler
$175.00
Digital Marketing

ADA
Development/ADA
$995.00   *
Digital Electronics Systems

ADA
Development/ADA
(48K) $250.00
Supersoft Associates

ADVENTURE
Games/Adventure
$24.95
Creative Computing
Software

ALGOL-60
Development/ALGOL
$199.00
Lifeboat Associates

AMCALL
Communications/
$95.00   *
Digital Marketing

AMETHYST
Word Processing/
Word Processing
(48K) $350.00
Mark of the Unicorn

ANALIZA
Games/Eliza
$35.00
Supersoft Associates

ANALYST
Develpment/List manager
(48K) $250.00
Structured Systems

ANGEL
Business/Time Management
$295.00
Time Management Software

APL/V80
Development/APL
$500.00
Lifeboat Associates

ASCOM
Communications/
$175.00
Westico

ASSEMBLER
Development/Assembler
Computer Products, Inc.

ASSEMBLER
Development/Assembler
Microsoft

ASSEMBLER
Development/Assembler
Midwest Micro-tek

BASIC B+
Development/DBMS
$325.00
Delphic Systems

BASIC COMPILER
Development/BASIC
Microsoft

BASIC UTILITY DISK
Utility/
$50.00
Lifeboat Associates

BASIC-80
Development/BASIC
$350.00
Microsoft

BAZIC
Development/BASIC
$150.00   *
Digital Marketing

BDS C COMPILER
Development/C
$145.00
Lifeboat Associates

BILL
Business/Energy
(64K) $295.00
Londe Parker Michels, Inc.

BSTAM
Communications/
$150.00
Lifeboat Associates

BSTMS
Communications/
$200.00
Lifeboat Associates

BT-80
Development/DBMS
(48K) $200.00
Digital Research

BUG
Development/Debugger
$129.00
Lifeboat Associates

BUSINESS SOFTWARE
Business/Accounting
Cybernetics

BUSINESS SOFTWARE
Business/Accounting
$150.00
Ontrak

BUSINESS SOFTWARE
Business/Accounting
Aaron Associates

BUSINESS SOFTWARE
Business/Accounting
Arkansas Systems

BUSINESS SOFTWARE
Business/Accounting
Cpaids

BUSINESS SOFTWARE
Business/Accounting
(56K)
Structured Systems

BUSINESS SOFTWARE
Business/Accounting
Peachtree Software

BUSINESS SOFTWARE
Business/Accounting
$675.00
End User Software

BUSINESS SOFTWARE
Business/Accounting
Software Hows

BUSINESS SOFTWARE
Business/Accounting
Micro Business Systems

BUSINESS SOFTWARE
Business/Accounting
Graham-Dorian Software
Systems

BUSINESS SOFTWARE
Business/Medical
Graham-Dorian Software
Systems

BUSINESS SOFTWARE
Business/Dental
Graham-Dorian Software
Systems

BUSINESS SOFTWARE
Business/Construction
Graham-Dorian Software
Systems

BUSINESS SOFTWARE
Business/Labor-Cost
Cal Data Systems

BUSINESS SOFTWARE
Business/Account Recv
Datasort, Inc.

BUSINESS SOFTWARE
Business/Accounting
Westware Systems II

C
Development/C
$200.00
Supersoft Associates

C
Development/C
(64K) $750.00
Whitesmiths

C COMPILER
Development/C
$75.00
The Code Works

C/80
Development/C
$39.95
Aardvark Software

CALCSTAR
Business/Worksheet
Micropro

CB80
Development/BASIC
Compiler Systems, Inc.

CBASIC2
Development/BASIC
$120.00　*
Digital Research

CBASIC2
Development/BASIC
Digital Research

CBS
Business/Accounting
$395.00
Lifeboat Associates

CIS COBOL
Development/COBOL
Micro Focus, Inc.

CLINK
Communications/
$75.00
Mycroft Labs

COMMUNICATIONS
SOFTWARE
Communications/
$60.00
Datastat Systems

COBOL-80
Development/COBOL
Microsoft

CONDOR SERIES
20/rDBMS
Development/DBMS
(48K)　$995.00
Condor Computer
Corporation

COPYPROOF
Word Processing/Spelling
$295.00　*
Digital Marketing

COPYWRITER
Word Processing/
Word Processing
$395.00
Digital Marketing

CP/M-86
Operating System/
Digital Research

CP/MODEM
Communications/
$300.00
Information Engineering

CP/NET
Operating System/
Digital Research

CROSS ASSEMBLERS
Development/
Crossassembler
$200.00
Avocet Systems

CROSS-COMPILE FORTH
Development/
Crosscompiler
Nautilus systems

CROSSTALK
Communications/
Microstuf, Inc.

CRTFORM
Word Processing/Editor
*
Statcom Corporation

DATA-VIEW
Business/Filing
$200.00
Supersoft Associates

DATASTAR
Business/Data Entry
$350.00
Micropro

DATAWRITE
Business/Accounting
Dataword, Inc.

DATEBOOK II
Business/Scheduling
(48K) $295.00   *
Digital Marketing

DBASE
Development/DBMS
(48K) $695.00
Ashton-Tate

DEB/ZEB
Development/Debugger
Infosoft

DENTAL BILLING
Business/Dental
$499.00
All Systems

DESPOOL
Utility/Spooler
Digital Research

DIAGNOSTICS II
Maintenance/
$100.00
Supersoft Associates

DICTION II
Word Processing/Dictionary
(60K) $195.00   *
Digital Marketing

DIF AND DEL
Utility/Disk
$45.00
Digital Constructs

DISK DOCTOR
Maintenance/Disk
$100.00
Supersoft Associates

DISK FIX
Utility/Disk
$150.00
Software Store

DISKCOPY
Utility/Disk
$37.50
Arkenstone

DISSAX
Development/Disassembler
(16K) $85.00
Cexec

DISTEL
Development/Disassembler
$65.00
Lifeboat Associates

DOCUMATE/PLUS
Word Processing/Indexing
$125.00   *
Orthocode Corporation

DPATCH
Maintenance/Disk
$195.00
Advanced Micro Techniques

DUNGEON MASTER
Games/D & D
$35.00
Supersoft Associates

EDIT
Word Processing/Editor
$129.00
Lifeboat Associates

EDIT-80
Word Processing/Editor
$89.00
Microsoft

EMERTUS PROPERTY
MANAGEMENT
Business/Property
*
Emertus

ESQ-1
Business/Legal
$1495.00
Lifeboat Associates

EXECUTIVE MAIL LIST
Business/Mailing List
(56K) $150.00
dilithium Software

FABS
Development/Indexing
$175.00   *
Digital Marketing

FIG FORTH
Development/FORTH
$95.00
Mitchell E. Timin
Engineering

FINANCIER
Business/Loans
Accountants Microsystems,
Inc.

FMS-80
Development/DBMS
Systems Plus

FORECASTER
Business/Financial Model
(48K) $250.00
Software Establishment

FORMS 2
Word Processing/
Screen Editor
$200.00
Lifeboat Associates

FORTH
Development/FORTH
$200.00
Supersoft Associates

FORTRAN IV
Development/FORTRAN
$100.00
Supersoft Associates

FORTRAN-80
Development/FORTRAN
$425.00
Microsoft

FPL
Business/Worksheet
(60K) $695.00
Lifeboat Associates

FRMFLEX
Word Processing/
Form Handling
(32K) $175.00
Cexec

GBS
Development/DBMS
$700.00
Quality Software

GAMES
Games/
Creative Computing
Software

GENERAL ON-LINE
DATABASE
Business/Accounting
Douthett Enterprises

GENESIS
Development/
Program Writing
$500
Time Management Software

GRAMMATIK
Word Processing/Grammar
$149.00   *
Aspen Software Company

GUARDIAN
Business/Time Management
$119.95
Time Management Software

I/SAL
Development/Assembler
*
Infosoft

IBM/CPM
Utility/
$175.00
Lifeboat Associates

IDM-C1
Development/DBMS
(60K) $159.00
Micro Architech Inc.

INCOPROP
Business/Income Property
EZ Software

INTERCHANGE
Development/Utilities
$59.95
Ecosoft

INVENTORY CONTROL
Business/Inventory
$995.00
Westico

INVENTORY CONTROL
SOFTWARE
Business/Inventory
$1000.00
Microcomputer Consultants

INVENTORY
MANAGEMENT
Business/Inventory
(32K) $250.00
dilithium Software

JANUS ADA
Development/ADA
(56K) $300.00
PR Software

JOB COST CONTROL
Business/Job Cost
$595.00
Westico

KBASIC
Development/DBMS
$435.00
Lifeboat Associates

KLH Spooler
Utility/Spooler
Tarbell Electronics

KSAM80
Development/ISAM
$395.00   *
Efficient Management
Systems

LEGAL BILLING
Business/Legal
$299.00
All Systems

LEGAL BILLING
Business/Legal
Micro Craft Inc.

LETTERRIGHT
Word Processing/Letters
(64K) $200.00
Structured Systems

LEVERAGE
Development/
Info Management
$185.00
Urban Software

LIFECOST
Business/Energy
(64K) $195.00
Londe Parker Michels, Inc.

LINKA
Development/Linker
Infosoft

LOGICALC
Business/Financial Model
$290.00
Software Products
International

LYNX
Development/Linker
$250.00
Westico

MAC
Development/Assembler
*
Digital Research

MAC
Development/Assembler
$90.00
Digital Research

MAC
Development/Assembler
Digital Research

MACRO-80
Development/Assembler
$149.00
Microsoft

MAGIC MENU
Word Processing/
Word Processing
(56K) $75.00 *
Digital Marketing

MAGIC WAND
Word Processing/
Word Processing
*
Small Business Applications

MAGSAM III
Development/DBMS
Micro Applications Group

MAILING LIST
Business/Mailing List
$219.00
Arkenstone

MAILING LIST
Business/Mailing list
$195.00
Digital Marketing

MAILMERGE
Word Processing/Mailing
*
Infosoft

MAPPER
Operating System/
$299.00
Omikron

MBASIC IV
Development/DBMS
(48K) $295.00
Micro Applications Group

MCALL
Communications/
$85.00 *
Digital Marketing

MDBS III
Development/DBMS
Micro Data Base
Systems, Inc.

MEDICAL BILLING
Business/Medical
$499.00
All Systems

MICRO B +
Development/DBMS
$260.00
Fair Com

MICRO-SEED
Development/DBMS
(48K) $1195.00 *
Micro Decisionware

MICRODENT
Business/Dental
*
Software Hows

MICROMED
Business/Medical
*
Software Hows

MICROPLAN
Business/Financial Model
$495.00   *
Standard Software
Corporation

MICROSPELL
Word Processing/Spelling
*
Lifeboat Associates

MICROSTAT
Research/Statistics
$250.00
Ecosoft

MICROTAX
Business/Tax
$1750.00
Microtax

MIDAS
Development/DBMS
Rothberg Information
Systems

MILESTONE
Business/PERT
(56K) $295.00   *
Digital Marketing

MINCE
Word Processing/Editor
Mark of the Unicorn

MONEY MAESTRO
Personal/Banking
(48K) $200.00
Innosys, Inc.

MULISP
Development/Lisp
$200.00
Microsoft

MUSIMP
Research/
$250.00
Microsoft

NAD
Business/Mailing List
$100.00
Lifeboat Associates

NEMESIS
Games/D & D
$35.00
Supersoft Associates

NEVADA COBOL
Development/COBOL
(16K) $149.95
Ellis Computing

NEVADA EDIT
Word Processing/Editor
(32K) $119.95
Ellis Computing

NEVADA PILOT
Development/Pilot
(32K) $149.95
Ellis Computing

NORTHSTAR BASIC
Development/BASIC
Infosoft

NPS-MICRO COBOL
Development/COBOL
(24K) $69.95
Software Review

NSBASIC INTERFACE
Development/BASIC
Infosoft

OPTIMUM
Development/DBMS
*
Uevon Computer
Systems, Inc.

OSBORNE BUSINESS
Business/Accounting
(48K) $59.00
Digital Systems

OVERHANG
Business/Energy
(64K) $195.00
Londe Parker Michels, Inc.

PALANTIR
Business/Accounting
*
Designer Software

PASCAL
Development/Pascal
$950.00
Whitesmiths

PASCAL/M
Development/Pascal
(56K) $225.00
Digital Marketing

PASCAL/MT +
Development/Pascal
(56K) $475.00
Mt Microsystems

PASCAL/Z
Development/Pascal
Intersystems

PASCALC
Business/Financial Model
$200.00   *
Concomp Industries

PASCODE 1
Business/Solar Design
(64K) $295.00
Londe Parker Michels, Inc.

PASM
Development/Assembler
$129.00
Lifeboat Associates

PBLC-DMN-1
Utility/
$15.00
Tarbell Electronics

PBLC-DMN-2
Utility/
$15.00
Tarbell Electronics

PEARL — LEVEL 2
Development/
Program Writing
$350.00   *
Digital Marketing

PEARL – LEVEL 3
Development/
Program Writing
$650.00 *
Digital Marketing

PEARL – LEVEL 1
Development/
Program Writing
$130.00 *
Digital Marketing

PERSONAL TAX
Business/Tax
(48K) $75.00
Aardvark Software

PL/I-80
Development/PL/I
*
Digital Research

PLAN80
Business/Financial Model
(56K) $295.00
Digital Marketing

PLINK
Communications/
$129.00
Lifeboat Associates

PMATE
Word Processing/Editor
$195.00
Lifeboat Associates

POSTMASTER
Business/Mailing List
$150.00
Lifeboat Associates

PRISM/LMS
Development/DBMS
$225.00 *
Micro Applications Group

PROFESSIONAL
MAILOUT
Business/Mailing List
(56K) $149.95
dilithium Software

PROGRAM MAP
Utility/
$150.00
Software Store

PROJECT
MANAGEMENT SYSTEM
Business/PERT
$995.00
North America Mica, Inc.

PROOFREADER
Word Processing/Spelling
$129.00 *
Aspen Software Company

QSORT
Business/Sort
$100.00
Lifeboat Associates

QUEST
Development/DBMS
$490.00
Software Products
International

QUICKSCREEN
Development/Screen Editor
$79.00
Fox and Geller Associates

RADAR
Word Processing/
Data Entry
Southern Computer Systems

RAID
Development/Debugger
$250.00
Lifeboat Associates

RATFOR
Development/Ratfor
$100.00
Supersoft Associates

RATFOR
Development/Ratfor
$39.95
Aardvark Software

RECLAIM
Utility/
$80.00
Lifeboat Associates

REFORMATTER
Development/
Disk Reformater
$195.00
Microtech Exports, Inc.

REMOTE
Communications/Control
Microstuf, Inc.

RM/COBOL
Development/COBOL
Cybernetics

ROOTS/M
Business/Genealogy
(32K) $124.95
Comm Soft

SCRATCHPAD
Business/Worksheet
$200.00
Supersoft Associates

SCRIBBLE
Word Processing/Editor
(48K) $125.00
Mark of the Unicorn

SELECT
Word Processing/
Word Processing
(48K) $595.00   *
Select Information Systems

SELECTOR IV
Development/DBMS
(56K) $550.00
Micro-Ap

SID
Development/Debugger
Digital Research

SMAL/80
Development/Assembler
Lifeboat Associates

SORT/B
Business/Sort
$75.00
Systemation

SPEED PROGRAMMING
PACKAGE
Development/Pascal
$475.00
Mt Microsystems

SPELLBINDER
Word Processing/Spelling
*
Lexisoft

SPELLGUARD
Word Processing/Spelling
(32K) $295.00
Innovative Software
Applications

SPELLSTAR
Word Processing/Spelling
(48K) *
Micropro

STANDARD TAX
Business/Tax
$495.00
Lifeboat Associates

STAR-EDIT
Word Processing/Editor
(32K) $225.00
Supersoft Associates

STATS-GRAPH
Business/Statistics
$200.00
Supersoft Associates

STOK PILOT
Development/
Operating System
$109.00
Stok Computer Interface

STRING/80
Utility/
Lifeboat Associates

SUPER M LIST
Word Processing/Mailing
$75.00
Supersoft Associates

SUPERCALC
Business/Worksheet
(48K) $295.00
Sorcim

SUPERSORT I
Business/Sorting
$250.00
Micropro

SUPERVYZ
Utility/Utility
$95.00
Epic Computer Corp.

T/MAKER
Business/Financial Model
$275.00
Lifeboat Associates

T/MAKER II
Business/Financial Model
$275.00 *
Lifeboat Associates

TARBELL BASIC
Development/BASIC
Tarbell Electronics

TARBELL DBMS
Development/DBMS
Tarbell Electronics

TASK
Business/Project Manage
$329.00 *
AMSI

TCS BUSINESS
Business/Accounting
$99.00
All Systems

TELECOM
Communications/
Tarbell Electronics

TERM
Communications/
$200.00
Supersoft Associates

TEX
Word Processing/
Word Processing
Digital Research

TEXTWRITER
Word Processing/
Word Processing
(32K)
Organic Software

TEXTWRITER III
Word Processing/
Word Processing
$125.00
Lifeboat Associates

TFS
Word Processing/Editor
$85.00
Supersoft Associates

THE BENCHMARK
Word Processing/
Word Processing
$499.00   *
R & B Computer Systems

THE BOOKKEEPER
SYSTEM
Business/Accounting
(64K)   *
Universal Software Studios

THE BOSS
Business/Accounting
$2495.00   *
Lifeboat Associates

THE ELECTRONIC
BLACKBOARD
Word Processing/
Word Processing
(48K) $198.00
Santa Cruz Software
Services

THE FINAL WORD
Word Processing/
Word Processing
(56K) $300.00
Mark of the Unicorn

THE FORMULA
Development/Report Gen
$595.00   *
Dynamic Microprocessor
Associate

THE PROGRAM
WRITER/REPORTER
Development/
Program Writing
$600.00
Vanloves/Vital Information,
Inc.

THE STRING BIT
Utility/
$65.00
Lifeboat Associates

THE WORD
Word Processing/Spelling
$75.00
Oasis Systems

TICKLER FILE/APPT.
CALENDAR
Business/Calendar
$95.00
Arkenstone

TINY C ONE
Development/C
$100.00   *
Tiny C. Associates

TINY C TWO
Development/C
$250.00   *
Tiny C Associates

TINY PASCAL
Development/Pascal
$85.00
Supersoft Associates

TRANS 86
Development/
Crosscompiler
(32K) $125.00   *
Digital Marketing

TEXTBOOK
Word Processing/
Word Processing
(40K) $100.00
Cexec

ULTRASORT
Business/Sort
$175.00   *
Digital Marketing

UNPROTECT
Utility/
$70.00
Systemation

UTILITIES
Development/Utilities
$60.00
Supersoft Associates

UTILITIES
Utility/
$24.95
Ficomp

UTILITIES
Utility/
Micah

V-COM DISASSEMBLER
Development/Disassembler
$80.00
Compuview Products

VEDIT
Word Processing/Editor
$130.00
Compuview Products

VSORT
Business/Sort
$175.00
Lifeboat Associates

WHATISIT
Development/DBMS
$175.00
Lifeboat Associates

WHITESMITHS C
COMPILER
Development/C
$630.00
Lifeboat Associates

WORD
Word Processing/
Word Processing
(64K) $75.00
Micro Architech Inc.

WORDMASTER
Word Processing/Editor
$150.00
Micropro

WORDSTAR
Word Processing/
Word Processing
(48K)
Micropro

WORKSHEET
Business/Whatif
(48K) $199.95
Soho Group

WPDAISY
Word Processing/
Word Processing
*
Infosoft

XASM
Development/
Crossassembler
$200.00
Lifeboat Associates

XLT86
Development/Translator
$150.00
Westico

XYBASIC
Development/BASIC
$450.00
Lifeboat Associates

Z-80 FORTH
Development/FORTH
(48K) $150.00
Laboratory Microsystems

Z8000 CROSSASSEMBLER
Development/
Crossassembler
$500.00
Supersoft Associates

CP/M SOFTWARE PRODUCT LISTING BY CATEGORY

Business/Account Recv.
   BUSINESS SOFTWARE   Datasort, Inc.
Business/Accounting
   BUSINESS SOFTWARE   Cybernetics
   BUSINESS SOFTWARE   Ontrak
   BUSINESS SOFTWARE   Aaron Associates
   BUSINESS SOFTWARE   Arkansas Systems
   BUSINESS SOFTWARE   Cpaids
   BUSINESS SOFTWARE   Structured Systems
   BUSINESS SOFTWARE   Peachtree Software
   BUSINESS SOFTWARE   End User Software

BUSINESS SOFTWARE	Software Hows
BUSINESS SOFTWARE	Micro Business Systems
BUSINESS SOFTWARE	Graham-Dorian Software Systems
BUSINESS SOFTWARE	Westware Systems II
ACCOUNTING PLUS	Systems Plus
CBS	Lifeboat Associates
DATAWRITE	Dataword, Inc.
GENERAL ON-LINE DATABASE	Douthett Enterprises
OSBORNE BUSINESS	Digital Systems
PALANTIR	Designer Software
TCS BUSINESS	All Systems
THE BOOKKEEPER SYSTEM	Universal Software Studios
THE BOSS	Lifeboat Associates

Business/Calendar

TICKLER FILE/ APPT. CALENDAR	Arkenstone

Business/Construction

BUSINESS SOFTWARE	Graham-Dorian Software Systems

Business/Data Entry

DATASTAR	Micropro

Business/Dental

BUSINESS SOFTWARE	Graham-Dorian Software Systems
DENTAL BILLING	All Systems
MICRODENT	Software Hows

Business/Energy

BILL	Londe Parker Michels, Inc.
LIFECOST	Londe Parker Michels, Inc.
OVERHANG	Londe Parker Michels, Inc.

Business/Filing

DATA-VIEW	Supersoft Associates

Business/Financial Model

FORECASTER	Software Establishment
LOGICALC	Software Products International
MICROPLAN	Standard Software Corporation
PASCALC	Concomp Industries

PLAN80	Digital Marketing
T/MAKER	Lifeboat Associates
T/MAKER II	Lifeboat Associates
Business/Genealogy	
ROOTS/M	Comm Soft
Business/Income Property	
INCOPROP	EZ Software
Business/Inventory	
INVENTORY CONTROL SOFTWARE	Microcomputer Consultants
INVENTORY CONTROL	Westico
INVENTORY MANAGEMENT	dilithium Software
Business/Job Cost	
JOB COST CONTROL	Westico
Business/Labor-Cost	
BUSINESS SOFTWARE	Cal Data Systems
Business/Legal	
ESQ-1	Lifeboat Associates
LEGAL BILLING	All Systems
LEGAL BILLING	Micro Craft Inc.
Business/Loans	
FINANCIER	Accountants Microsystems, Inc.
Business/Mailing List	
EXECUTIVE MAILLIST	dilithium Software
MAILING LIST	Arkenstone
MAILING LIST	Digital Marketing
NAD	Lifeboat Associates
POSTMASTER	Lifeboat Associates
PROFESSIONAL MAILOUT	dilithium Software
Business/Medical	
BUSINESS SOFTWARE	Graham-Dorian Software Systems
MEDICAL BILLING	All Systems
MICROMED	Software Hows
Business/PERT	
MILESTONE	Digital Marketing
PROJECT MANAGEMENT SYSTEM	North America Mica, Inc.

Business/Project Manage
  TASK   AMSI
Business/Property
  EMERTUS PROPERTY   Emertus
    MANAGEMENT
Business/Scheduling
  DATEBOOK II   Digital Marketing
Business/Solar Design
  PASCODE 1   Londe Parker Michels, Inc.
Business/Sort
  QSORT   Lifeboat Associates
  SORT/B   Systemation
  ULTRASORT   Digital Marketing
  VSORT   Lifeboat Associates
Business/Sorting
  SUPERSORT I   Micropro
Business/Statistics
  STATS-GRAPH   Supersoft Associates
Business/Tax
  MICROTAX   Microtax
  PERSONAL TAX   Aardvark Software
  STANDARD TAX   Lifeboat Associates
Business/Time Management
  ANGEL   Time Management Software
  GUARDIAN   Time Management Software
Business/What If
  WORKSHEET   Soho Group
Business/Worksheet
  CALCSTAR   Micropro
  FPL   Lifeboat Associates
  SCRATCHPAD   Supersoft Associates
  SUPERCALC   Sorcim
Communications/
  COMMUNICATIONS   Datastat Systems
    SOFTWARE
  AMCALL   Digital Marketing
  ASCOM   Westico
  BSTAM   Lifeboat Associates
  BSTMS   Lifeboat Associates
  CLINK   Mycroft Labs
  CP/MODEM   Information Engineering

CROSSTALK	Microstuf, Inc.
MCALL	Digital Marketing
PLINK	Lifeboat Associates
TELECOM	Tarbell Electronics
TERM	Supersoft Associates
Communications/Control	
REMOTE	Microstuf, Inc.
Development/ADA	
ADA	Digital Electronics Systems
ADA	Supersoft Associates
JANUS ADA	PR Software
Development/ALGOL	
ALGOL-60	Lifeboat Associates
Development/APL	
APL/V80	Lifeboat Associates
Development/Assembler	
(ASSEMBLER)	Computer Products, Inc.
(ASSEMBLER)	Microsoft
(ASSEMBLER)	Midwest Micro-Tek
(MAC)	Digital Research
I/SAL	Infosoft
MAC	Digital Research
MAC	Digital Research
MACRO-80	Microsoft
PASM	Lifeboat Associates
SMAL/80	Lifeboat Associates
Development/BASIC	
BASIC COMPILER	Microsoft
BASIC-80	Microsoft
BAZIC	Digital Marketing
CB80	Compiler Systems, Inc.
CBASIC2	Digital Research
CBASIC2	Digital Research
NORTHSTAR BASIC	Infosoft
NSBASIC INTERFACE	Inforsoft
TARBELL BASIC	Tarbell Electronics
XYBASIC	Lifeboat Associates
Development/C	
BDS C COMPILER	Lifeboat Associates
C	Supersoft Associates
C	Whitesmiths
C COMPILER	The Code Works

C/80	Aardvark Software
TINY C ONE	Tiny C Associates
TINY C TWO	Tiny C Associates
WHITESMITHS C COMPILER	Lifeboat Associates

Development/COBOL

CIS COBOL	Micro Focus, Inc.
COBOL-80	Microsoft
NEVADA COBOL	Ellis Computing
NPS-MICRO COBOL	Software Review
RM/COBOL	Cybernetics

Development/Crossassembler

CROSS ASSEMBLERS	Avocet Systems
XASM	Lifeboat Associates
Z8000 CROSSASSEMBLER	Supersoft Associates

Development/Crosscompiler

CROSS-COMPILE FORTH	Nautilus Systems
TRANS 86	Digital Marketing

Development/DBMS

BASIC B +	Delphic Systems
BT-80	Digital Research
CONDOR SERIES 20/rDBMS	Condor Computer Corporation
DBASE	Ashton-Tate
FMS-80	Systems Plus
GBS	Quality Software
IDM-C1	Micro Architech Inc.
KBASIC	Lifeboat Associates
MAGSAM III	Micro Applications Group
MBASIC IV	Micro Applications Group
MDBS III	Micro Data Base Systems, Inc.
MICRO B +	Fair Com
MICRO-SEED	Micro Decisionware
MIDAS	Rothberg Information Systems
OPTIMUM	Uevon Computer Systems, Inc.
PRISM/LMS	Micro Applications Group
QUEST	Software Products International
SELECTOR IV	Micro-Ap

TARBELL DBMS	Tarbell Electronics
WHATISIT	Lifeboat Associates

Development/Debugger

BUG	Lifeboat Associates
DEB/ZEB	Infosoft
RAID	Lifeboat Associates
SID	Digital Research

Development/Disassembler

DISSAX	Cexec
DISTEL	Lifeboat Associates
V-COM DISASSEMBLER	Compuview Products

Development/Disk Reformatter

REFORMATTER	Microtech Exports, Inc.

Development/FORTH

FIG FORTH	Michell E. Timin Engineering
FORTH	Supersoft Associates
Z-80 FORTH	Laboratory Microsystems

Development/Fortran

FORTRAN IV	Supersoft Associates
FORTRAN-80	Microsoft

Development/Indexing

FABS	Digital Marketing

Development/Info Management

LEVERAGE	Urban Software

Development/ISAM

KSAM80	Efficient Management Systems

Development/Linker

LINKA	Infosoft
LYNX	Westico

Development/LISP

MULISP	Microsoft

Development/List Manager

ANALYST	Structured systems

Development/Macro Assembler

ACT I	Digital Marketing
ACT II	Digital Marketing

Development/Operating System

STOK PILOT	Stok Computer Interface

Development/Pascal

PASCAL	Whitesmiths
PASCAL/M	Digital Marketing

PASCAL MT +	Mt Microsystems
PASCAL/Z	Intersystems
SPEED PROGRAMMING PACKAGE	Mt Microsystems
TINY PASCAL	Supersoft Associates
Development/PILOT	
NEVADA PILOT	Ellis Computing
Development/PL/I	
PL/I-80	Digital Research
Development/Program Writing	
GENESIS	Time Management Software
PEARL – LEVEL 2	Digital Marketing
PEARL – LEVEL 3	Digital Marketing
PEARL – LEVEL 1	Digital Marketing
THE PROGRAM WRITER/REPORTER	Vanloves/Vital Information, Inc.
Development/Ratfor	
RATFOR	Supersoft Associates
RATFOR	Aardvark Software
Development/Report Gen	
THE FORMULA	Dynamic Microprocessor Associate
Development/RPG	
ACCESS/80	Friends Software
Development/Screen Editor	
QUICKSCREEN	Fox and Geller Associates
Development/Translator	
XLT86	Westico
Development/Utilities	
INTERCHANGE	Ecosoft
UTILITIES	Supersoft Associates
Games/	
GAMES	Creative Computing Software
Games/Adventure	
ADVENTURE	Creative Computing Software
Games/D & D	
DUNGEON MASTER	Supersoft Associates
NEMESIS	Supersoft Associates
Games/Eliza	
ANALIZA	Supersoft Associates
Maintenance/	
DIAGNOSTICS II	Supersoft Associates

Maintenance/Disk
DISK DOCTOR	Supersoft Associates
DPATCH	Advanced Micro Techniques

Operating System/
CP/M-86	Digital Research
CP/NET	Digital Research
MAPPER	Omikron

Personal/Banking
MONEY MAESTRO	Innosys, Inc.

Research/
MUSIMP	Microsoft

Research/Statistics
ABSTAT	Anderson-Bell Company
MICROSTAT	Ecosoft

Utility/
UTILITIES	Ficomp
UTILITIES	Micah
BASIC UTILITY DISK	Lifeboat Associates
IBM/CPM	Lifeboat Associates
PBLC-DMN-1	Tarbell Electronics
PBLC-DMN-2	Tarbell Electronics
PROGRAM MAP	Software Store
RECLAIM	Lifeboat Associates
STRING/80	Lifeboat Associates
THE STRING BIT	Lifeboat Associates
UNPROTECT	Systemation

Utility/Disk
DIF AND DEL	Digital Contructs
DISK FIX	Software Store
DISKCOPY	Arkenstone

Utility/Spooler
DESPOOL	Digital Research
KLH Spooler	Tarbell Electronics

Utility/Utility
SUPERVYZ	Epic Computer Corp.

Word Processing/Data Entry
RADAR	Southern Computer Systems

Word Processing/Dictionary
DICTION II	Digital Marketing

Word Processing/Editor
CRTFORM	Statcom Corporation
EDIT	Lifeboat Associates

EDIT-80	Microsoft
MINCE	Mark of the Unicorn
NEVADA EDIT	Ellis Computing
PMATE	Lifeboat Associates
SCRIBBLE	Mark of the Unicorn
STAR-EDIT	Supersoft Associates
TFS	Supersoft Associates
VEDIT	Compuview Products
WORDMASTER	Micropro
Word Processing/Form Handling	
FRMFLEX	Cexec
Word Processing/Grammar	
GRAMMATIK	Aspen Software Company
Word Processing/Indexing	
DOCUMATE/PLUS	Orthocode Corporation
Word Processing/Letters	
LETTERRIGHT	Structured Systems
Word Processing/Mailing	
MAILMERGE	Infosoft
SUPER M LIST	Supersoft Associates
Word Processing/Screen Editor	
FORMS 2	Lifeboat Associates
Word Processing/Spelling	
COPYPROOF	Digital Marketing
MICROSPELL	Lifeboat Associates
PROOFREADER	Aspen Software Company
SPELLBINDER	Lexisoft
SPELLGUARD	Innovative Software Applications
SPELLSTAR	Microrpo
THE WORD	Oasis Systems
Word Processing/Word Processing	
AMETHYST	Mark of the Unicorn
COPYWRITER	Digital Marketing
MAGIC MENU	Digital Marketing
MAGIC WAND	Small Business Applications
SELECT	Select information Systems
TEX	Digital Research
TEXTWRITER	Organic Software
TEXWRITER III	Lifeboat Associates
THE BENCHMARK	R & B Computer Systems

THE ELECTRONIC BLACKBOARD	Santa Cruz Software Services
THE FINAL WORD	Mark of the Unicorn
TXTBOOK	Cexec
WORD	Micro Architech Inc.
WORDSTAR	Micropro
WPDAISY	Infosoft

CP/M SOFTWARE VENDORS

Aardvark Software
783 North Water Street
Milwaukee, WI 53202
(414) 289-9988

Aaron Associates
Box 170A
Garden Grove, CA 92640

Accountants
Microsystems, Inc.
121 N. Louis St.
La Habra, CA 90631

Advanced Micro Techniques
1291 E. Hillsdale Blvd., #209
Foster City, CA 94404
(415) 349-9336

All Systems
332 East 30th Street
New York, NY 10016
(800) 221-2486

AMSI
1935 Cliff Valley Wy, NE,
Suite 200
Atlanta, GA 30329
(404) 634-9535

Anderson-Bell Company
2916 S. Stuart Street
Denver, CO 80236

Arkansas Systems
Suite 206, 8901 Kanis Rd.
Little Rock, AR 72205
(501) 227-8471

Arkenstone
870 Market Street, Suite 369
San Francisco, CA 94102

Ashton-Tate
9929 West Jefferson Blvd.
Culver City, CA 90230
(213) 204-5570

Aspen Software Company
PO Box 339-W
Tijeras, NM 87059
(505) 281-1634

Avocet Systems
804 South State St.
Dover, DE 19901
(302) 734-0151

Cal Data Systems
150 Felker Street, Suite B
Santa Cruz, CA 95060

Cexec
211 Sutter Street, Suite 300
San Francisco, CA 94108
(415) 981-4724

Chang Laboratories
10228 North Stelling Road
Cupertino, CA 95014
(408) 725-8088

Comm Soft
665 Maybell Avenue
Palo Alto, CA 94306
(415) 493-2184

Compiler Systems, Inc.
37 N. Auburn Ave.
Sierra Madre, CA 91024
(213) 355-1063

Computer Products, Inc.
PO Box 805
Mesa, AZ 85202

Compuview Products
618 Louise
Ann Arbor, MI 48103
(313) 996-1299

Concomp Industries
8338 Center Drive
La Mesa, CA 92041
(714) 464-6373

Condor Computer
Corporation
3989 Research Park Dr.
Ann Arbor, MI 48107
(313) 769-3988

Cpaids
1640 Franklin Ave.
Kent, OH 44240
(800) 321-2430

Creative Computing
Software
39 E. Hanover St.
Morris Plains, NJ 07950
(800) 631-8112

Cybernetics
8041 Newman Ave.
Suite 208
Huntington Beach, CA 92647
(714) 848-1922

Datasort, Inc.
3237 Claremont Way
Suite 202
Napa, CA 94558

Datastat Systems
631 B St.
San Diego, CA 92101

Dataword, Inc.
1404 140th Pl., NE
Bellevue, WA 98007
(206) 643-2050

Delphic Systems
2260 Compton Ave.
St. Louis, MO 63104

Designer Software
3400 Montrose Blvd.
Houston, TX 77006
(713) 520-8221

Digital Contructs
130 East Main Street
Norristown, PA 19401
(215) 279-5652

Digital Electronics Systems
Box 5252
Torrance, CA 90510
(213) 539-6239

Digital Marketing
2670 Cherry Lane
Walnut Creek, CA 94596
(415) 938-2880

Digital Research
801 Lighthouse Ave.
Pacific Grove, CA 93950

Digital Systems
4301 Montana
El Paso, TX 79903
(915) 566-8655

dilithium Software
11000 SW 11th St., Suite E
Beaverton, OR 97005
(503) 646-2713

Douthett Enterprises
906 N. Main
Wichita, KA 67203

Dynamic Microprocessor
Associate
545 Fifth Ave.
New York, NY 10017
(212) 687-7115

Ecosoft
PO Box 68602
Indianapolis, IN 46268
(317) 283-8883

Efficient Management
Systems
3645 Grand Ave., Suite 304
Oakland, CA 94610

Ellis Computing
600 41st Ave.
San Francisco, CA 94121
(415) 751-1522

Emertus
1932 South Karen Ave.
Fresno, CA 93727
(209) 251-3525

End User Software
150 Felker Street
Santa Cruz, CA 95060

Epic Computer Corp.
9181 Chesapeake Dr.
San Diego, CA 92123
(714) 569-0440

EZ Software
PO Box 591
Novato, CA 94947

Fair Com
2606 Johnson Drive
Columbia, MO 65201
(314) 445-3304

Ficomp
3017 Talking Rock Dr.
Farfax, VA 22031

Fox and Geller Associates
PO Box 1053
Teaneck, NJ 07666
(201) 837-0142

Friends Software
Tioga Building, Suite 440
Berkeley, CA 94701
(415) 540-7282

Graham-Dorian Software
Systems
5316 Trail Lake Drive
Fort Worth, TX 76133
(817) 294-2510

Information Engineering
8 Bay Rd.
New Market, NH 03857
(603) 659-5891

Infosoft
25 Sylvan Road South
Westport, CT 06880
(203) 226-8937

Innosys, Inc.
2150 Shattuck Ave.
Berkeley, CA 94704
(415) 843-8122

Innovative Software
Applications
Box 2797
Menlo Park, CA 94205
(415) 326-0805

Intersystems
1650 Hanshaw Rd.
Ithica, NY 14850
(607) 257-0190

Laboratory Microsystems
4147 Beethoven Street
Los Angeles, CA 90066
(213) 390-9292

Lexisoft
Box 267
Davis, CA 95616
(916) 758-3630

Lifeboat Associates
2248 Broadway
New York, NY 10024

Londe Parker Michels, Inc.
150 N. Meramac
St. Louis, MO 83105
(314) 725-5501

Mark of the Unicorn
PO Box 423
Arlington, MA 02174
(617) 489-1387

Metasoft Corporation
711 E. Cottonwood Lane
Suite E
Casa Grande, AZ 85222
(602) 836-6160

Micah
Box 4987
Walnut Creek, CA 94596
(415) 933-2783

Micro Applications Group
7300 Caldus Ave.
Van Nuys, CA 90146

Micro Architech Inc.
96 Dothan St.
Arlington, MA 02174
(617) 643-4713

Micro Business Systems
6401 Roosevelt Way NE
Seattle, WA 98115

Micro Craft Inc.
1001 Hickory Lane
Huntsville, AL 35803
(205) 883-1817

Micro Data Base
Systems, Inc.
Box 248
Lafayette, IN 47902
(317) 448-1616

Micro Decisionware
4890 Riverbend Rd.
Boulder, CO 80301
(303) 443-2760

Micro Focus, Inc.
1601 Civic Center Drive
Santa Clara, CA 95050
(408) 984-6961

Micro-Ap
9807 Davona Dr.
San Ramon, CA 94583
(415) 828-6697

Microcomputer Consultants
PO Box T
Davis, CA 95617
(916) 756-8104

Micropro
1299 4th Street
San Rafael, CA 94901

Microsoft
400 108th NE, Suite 200
Bellevue, WA 98004
(206) 455-8080

Microstuf, Inc.
Box 33337
Decatur, CA 30033
(404) 491-3787

Microtax
22713 Ventura Blvd., Suite F
Woodland Hills, CA 91364
(213) 704-7800

Microtech Exports, Inc.
467 Hamilton Ave., Suite 2
Palo Alto, CA 94301
(415) 324-9114

Midwest Micro-Tek
PO Box 29411
Brooklyn Ctr., MN 55429

Mitchell E. Timin
Engineering
9575 Genesee Ave., Suite E2
San Diego, CA 92121
(714) 455-9008

Mt. Microsystems
1562 Kings Cross Drive
Cardiff, CA 92007
(714) 753-4856

Mycroft Labs
PO Box 6045
Tallahasee, FL 32301

Nautilus Systems
PO Box 1098
Santa Cruz, CA 95061

North America Mica, Inc.
11772 Sorrento Valley Rd.
#240
San Diego, CA 92121

Oasis Systems
2765 Reynard Way
San Diego, CA 92103
(714) 291-9489

Omikron
1127 Hearst St.
Berkeley, CA 94702
(415) 845-8013

Ontrak
PO Box 2134
Yorba Linda, CA 92686
(714) 993-0142

Oregon Professional
Microsystems
4110 NE Alameda
Portland, OR 97212
(503) 282-5835

Organic Software
1492 Windsor Way
Livermore, CA 94550
(415) 455-4034

Orthocode Corporation
PO Box 6191
Albany, CA 94706
(415) 527-9300

Peachtree Software
Suite 700, 3 Corporate Sq.
Atlanta, GA 30329
(404) 325-8533

PR Software
PO Box 1512
Madison, WI 53701
(608) 244-6436

Quality Software
6660 Reseda Blvd., Suite 105
Reseda, CA 91335
(213) 344-6599

R & B Computer Systems
1954 E. University
Tempe, AZ 85281
(800) 528-7385

Rothberg Information
Systems
260 Sheridan Ave.
Palo Alto, CA 94306

Santa Cruz Software
Services
1711 Quail Hollow Rd.
Lomond, CA 95005
(408) 336-2170

Select Information Systems
919 Sir Francis Drake Blvd.
Kentfield, CA 94904
(415) 459-4003

Small Business Applications
3220 Louisiana, Suite 205
Houston, TX 77006
(713) 528-5158

Software Establishment
705A Lakefield Rd.
Westlake Village, CA 91361
(213) 991-7711

Software Hows
PO Box 36275
Los Angeles, CA 90036
(213) 731-0876

Software Products
International
5482 Complex Street
Suite 115
San Diego, CA 92123
(714) 268-4346

Software Review
704 Solano Ave.
Albany, CA 94704
(415) 527-7730

Software Store
706 Chippewa Square
Marquette, MI 49855
(906) 228-7622

Soho Group
140 Thompson St., Suite 4-B
New York, NY 10012

Sorcim
405 Aldo Ave.
Santa Clara, CA 95051
(408) 248-5543

Southern Computer Systems
PO Box 3373A
Birmingham, AL 35255
(205) 933-1659

Standard Software
Corporation
10 Mazzeo Drive
Randolph, MA 02368
(617) 963-7220

Statcom Corporation
5766 Balcones Suite 202
Austin, TX 78731
(512) 451-0221

Stok Computer Interface
PO Box 501
Woodside, NY 11377
(212) 426-7022

Structured Systems
5204 Claremont
Oakland, CA 94618
(415) 547-1567

Supersoft Associates
PO Box 1628
Champaign, IL 61820
(217) 344-7596

Systemation
PO Box 75
Richton Park, IL 60471
(312) 481-2420

Systems Plus
3975 East Bayshore
Palo Alto, CA 94303
(415) 969-7047

Tarbell Electronics
950 Dovlen Place, Suite B
Carson, CA 90746
(213) 538-4251

The Code Works
Box 550
Goleta, CA 93116
(805) 683-1585

Time Management Software
123 E. Broadway
Cushing, OK 74023
(800) 824-7888

Tiny C Associates
PO Box 269
Holmdel, NJ 07733
(201) 671-2296

Uevon Computer
Systems, Inc.
899 Logan Street
Denver, CO 80203
(800) 525-1637

Universal Software Studios
179 West Smith Street
Gallatin, TN 37066
(615) 452-1027

Urban Software
19 West 34th Street
New York, NY 10001
(212) 947-3811

Vanloves/Vital
Information, Inc.
7899 Mastin Dr.
Overland Park, KS 66204
(800) 255-5119

Westico
25 Van Zant Street
Norwalk, CT 06855
(203) 853-6880

Westware Systems II
2455 SW 4th Ave.
Ontario, OR 97914
(503) 881-1477

Whitesmiths
PO Box 1132,
Ansonia Station
New York, NY 10023
(212) 799-1200

APPENDIX D

CP/M Diagnostics

PROBLEM	CAUSE	SOLUTION
CP/M does not come up. With disk drive cover removed, head does not load to disk.	Disk inserted incorrectly. Hardware problems.	Insert disk correctly. Check disk cables, drive, and disk controller.
CP/M does not come up. With disk drive cover removed, head loads but does not move across disk.	Problems with SBOOT program, wrong memory size or bad CPU or memory (first page).	Check lowest page of memory, SBOOT, CPU.
CP/M does not come up. With disk drive cover removed head loads and moves very slightly across disk. No display on video.	Wrong port numbers or jumps in CONOT of BIOS, bad upper memory.	Stop computer and examine memory where system is stopped. If in CONOT, change port or jump instructions. Check upper memory.

CP/M does not come up. Some video displayed, but text is garbage.	Problems in video terminal, baud rates of terminal or I/O card, or jump instructions in CONOT of BIOS.	Check video terminal switches and CONOT of BIOS.
CRC error messages or write error messages.	Bad disks, dirty disk head or bad head alignment.	Try different disk, do disk tests, clean head with alcohol. If this doesn't work, get disk alignment checked.
Read error messages.	Bad disks, dirty disk head or bad head alignment.	Do disk test, clean heads, check alignment if these do not work.
Disk does rhythmic head load and unload continuously. Control/C does not stop cycle.	Disk has run out of storage space, and BIOS or program did not recover properly.	Reboot system. Check storage space. Remember editor and PIP require .$$$ files with as much space as original file. Clear off unused files as BAK files and try again.
System locks up and freezes on a call to printer.	Printer is not turned on.	Turn printer on.
System locks up and freezes. No printer call was issued.	Hardware problems in CPU or memory.	Check memory and CPU.
	Printer not turned on.	Turn printer on.

Assembler generates error messages even though source file is correct. Error messages indicate source file is not correct.	Poorly designed memory cards are loading the bus in the computer too much or memory is bad.	Minimize memory size to only what is necessary to compile. Check memory.
Computer hung in disk or print cycle and control/c doesn't seem to stop anything.		Stop system with control/s, then use control/c.
R/O error message.	Disks were changed without a warm start.	Whenever disks are changed, a warm start (control/c) must be done, or a RESET before change if BASIC is being used. Warm start and try again.

APPENDIX E

CP/M User Groups

One of the most remarkable sources of programs for CP/M users is the CP/M User's Group. Started by Tony Gold of the Lifeboat Associates address, this group has 76 different disk volumes available at $8 each with a catalog available for $6.

There is no restriction on copying these disks, and often computer clubs in cities order a set and local club members copy programs as they are needed. Another alternative is to locate a few local CP/M users, order most of the set, and split the cost. Each person copies those programs he needs and then the disks are stored at a bank deposit box.

The disks include utility programs, games, documentation on undocumented features of CP/M, and application programs. Some of the software is high quality, some will have little value to many. You will have fun searching these disks for treasures for your own use.

You can also help the user group by contributing your own software and creativity. If the programs help you, help others by sending the group your own programs that you develop.

CP/M User's Group
1651 Third Avenue
New York, NY 10028

CP/M USER GROUP

Volume	Description
1	CP/M Utilities
2	Lawrence Livermore BASIC
3	BASIC E Games
4	ACTOR Interpreter and FORTRAN Random Number Subroutines
5	Mixed Games
6	Chicago Area Computer Hobbyist Exchange Programs (Mailing List Program)
7	PILOT
8	Utilities
9	General Ledger Program
10	Lawrence Livermore BASIC (Updated)
11	Disk Tiny BASIC and PT BASIC/5
12	PILOT (Update)
13	Mixed Games
14	CP/M Utilities
15	Utilities and Non-BASIC Games
16	Utilities, FOCAL
17	Utilities, Denver Tiny BASIC, Games
18	Math Routines
19	Utilities
20	BASIC E Games
21	Microsoft BASIC Games
22	Monster Startrek Games
23	STOIC Compiler
24	CP/M utilities, macrolibraries, RATFOR
25	Utilities, modem software, disk catalog system
26	Microsoft BASIC Games
27	Microsoft BASIC Games
28	Tarbell Data Base System and Algol-like Language
29	Assembler Games, Some BASIC E Source
30	BASIC E PLM Source
31	Tarbell BASIC and Source (Part I)
32	Tarbell BASIC Source (Part II)
33	Search and Rescue Programs
34	SAM 76 Language
35	FELIX Graphics Animation System
36	Assemblers and Editors

37	CBASIC2 Programs
38	CP/M Speed-up Utilities and Tarbell Controller Utilities
39	Music Programs
40	Utilities (Modem, DU, Cataloging)
41	Ham Radio Programs
42	Disassemblers
43	Osborne A/P
44	Osborne G/L
45	Osborne Payroll
46	Modem Programs and Utilities
47	Modem Programs
48	BDOS C Programs
49	CDOS Disk and RATFOR
50	Pascal Compiler
51	Stage 2 Microprocessor
52	Copyfast and Other Utilities
53	BDOS-C Adventure
54	MBASIC Games
55	Original Adventure (run time)
56	Original Adventure (source)
57	Expanded Adventure (run time)
58	CP/M Utilities
59	Diagnostics
60	6502 Simulator
61	Bulletin Board Software
62	Pascal and Communication Software
63	Utilities
64	Games, Disassembler
65	FIG-FORTH
66	HELP System
67	User Group Catalog
68	Utilities
69	Utilities
70	Utilities
71	Pascal Z Programs
72	PCE System Monitor
73	Pascal Z Utilities
74	Pascal Z Utilities
75	MBASIC Disassembler
76	Pascal Z Utilities

77   Dr. Bowles Database Seed Program
78   Utilities
79   Modem Programs

Other User Groups

Amethyst User Group
Barry Dobyns
1633 Royal Creat #1128
Austin, TX 78741

BDOS-C User Group
Box 287
Yates Center, KS 66783

DBASE User Group
PO Box 7443
Riverside, CA 92503

Osborne Business Software User Group
2256 Main Street, Suite 11
Otay, CA 92011

Pascal/Z User Group
7962 Center Parkway
Sacramento, CA 95823

PL/I User Group
Digital Research
Box 579
Pacific Grove, CA 93950

SIG/M
Box 97
Iselin, NJ 08830

APPENDIX F

Glossary

addressable cursor—a video cursor whose position can be moved by software.

APL (A Programming Language)—a high-level programming language primarily used for list and array processing. Highly compact source language with special symbols and often requires a special keyboard and printer.

application program—a program for a particular use such as a word processor, general ledger, or mailing list processor.

ASCII (American National Standard Code for Information Interchange)—a standard code of seven or eight bits used for information exchange between computer systems.

ASCII files—data files consisting entirely of ASCII characters, as a letter file for a word processing program.

assemble—to translate a program from assembly language to computer machine language.

assembler—a computer program that converts a program in a symbolic language to an executable form in machine language. The CP/M assembler converts a source program to a HEX file form, and requires the LOAD program to convert this to an executable form.

assembly-level program—a program in a language in which the instructions usually have a one-to-one correspondence with the computer instructions. Such a program is highly specific to a particular type of microprocessor (as 8080 or 6502) and requires extensive modifications to use on another type of system.

baud rate — the transmission rate of information between computers, refers to the bit transmission rate. A fast selectric is roughly 150 baud, and a low speed modem used in microprocessor systems is 300 baud. Video terminals used as a console are normally 4800 or 9600 baud.

BDOS (Basic Disk Operating System) — the CP/M routines for the management of the disk writing and reading. The routines are hardware independent.

binary system — a numeric system in which each symbol represents a power of two.

BIOS (Basic I/O System) — the module of CP/M that contains all the input and output routines for all the peripherals. This is the only part of CP/M that is hardware dependent.

BIOS software driver — an I/O routine in the BIOS module, as the printer driver.

bootstrap — a short computer program used to load a longer program.

byte — a binary character, generally eight bits in a microprocessor.

bus (or buss) — one or more conductors for the transmission of signals or power.

CCP (Console Command Processor) — the console command processor of CP/M that interprets keyboard commands.

character commands — editor functions that reference particular characters within a line as the *D* and *C* commands.

character generator circuits — those electronic circuits within a video terminal that create the characters on the screen that correspond with the ASCII input codes from the computer.

COBOL — (Common Business-Oriented Language) — a high level program specifically for business applications.

COM files — CP/M program files on the disk that are machine-level language and which can be directly loaded and executed.

command mode – an editor input phase in which input is interpreted as an order.

compiler – a program that converts a program from a high level language to a computer or machine oriented language.

complex commands – editor functions that can do multiple operations as the *J* and *M* commands.

console – a part of the computer system used for communication between the user and the system. Generally includes a keyboard and video display.

control commands – editor functions that set up parameters for the editor operation, such as the *V* command.

core – a word used to refer to the computer memory. Older computer memories were made of ferrite cores. These have been replaced with integrated circuits in modern computers.

cursor – a movable visible mark used to indicate position on a video screen.

data – a representation of information in a form suitable for processing by computers.

data base – a set of data consisting of at least one file and sufficient for a given purpose in a computer system. A collection of information in a formal form.

data file – collected information on the disk used by a program for processing (contrast to program files).

daughter board – an electronic circuit board that is installed as a component of another larger board (mother board).

debug – to detect, trace, or eliminate mistakes in a computer program.

decimal system – a number system in which each digit represents a power of ten.

device assignments – the relationship of the logical devices to the physical devices used in a computer system.

directory – an index used by a control program to locate one or more blocks of data on a disk.

directory information – information concerning the file locations, lengths, and sizes. Normally stored on track 3 of a diskette in a CP/M system.

disk controller – the hardware used to manage the disk operation.

diskette (disk) – a thin magnetic disk in a semi-rigid protective jacket.

dynamic file allocation – managing disk space in such a way so that if files are deleted or altered, disk space is automatically allocated and recovered without having to repack the information on the disk.

dynamic memory – memory in which information is physically stored only a short time, and must be physically rewritten periodically by support circuits. Most microcomputer systems now use dynamic memory, and information is automatically rewritten in such circuits many times a second.

editor – a program that creates and alters text files.

extent – the maximum amount of disk space that can be allocated by a single CP/M directory entry. The CP/M extent size is 16K (16,384 bytes), and if a file requires more space than this CP/M will automatically create additional directory entries. Most directory listings (as DIR) will show all file extents as a single directory entry.

FDOS – the combined BDOS/BIOS modules of CP/M.

file commands – editor functions that are used to open, close, read, and write files as the *E*, *H*, and *O* commands.

file – a collection of related records treated as a single item.

file transfers – the act of moving a collection of related items identified as a unit from one place (as the disk) to another (as a second disk).

firmware – computer hardware with information content value, as a PROM with a program stored within its memory.

formatter – a program that controls the output image of a text file and normally can page, justify, and otherwise image the output.

FORTRAN (formula translation) — a high level language used primarily for scientific applications.

graphic display — a pictorial representation of information, normally on a video terminal.

hardware — computer resources with physical visibility (contrasts with firmware and software).

head — the device that reads, writes, or erases information on a storage medium such as a diskette.

hexadecimal — a number system in which each symbol represents a power of sixteen. Sixteen values are required for each digit (0-9, A-F).

high resolution — refers to a display or printout in which the characters or symbols are composed of a large number of independent parts. A high resolution display displays a large amount of information as compared with a low resolution display.

input mode — an editor input phase in which input is interpreted as text.

interpreter — a program that resides in the computer memory with the application program and translates the program to a machine level language on a statement-by-statement basis as the application program is used.

I/O — pertaining to a device or channel that may be involved in an input process and, at another time, in an output process.

justify — to control the printing position of the characters on a page so that the left-hand and right-hand margins or the printout are regular.

kernel — that part of the operating system that always remains in the computer memory.

keyboard — a device for sending data by key depression in which the keys, when pressed, generate defined codes (as ASCII).

line command — editor functions that act on an entire line of text to add, modify, and delete lines of text.

listing — a printout of the source language statements of a program.

LOAD program — a program that converts CP/M files stored in HEX format to a machine-level COM program file.

logical device — a peripheral referenced by a computer program. Some CP/M systems can use STAT to control the relationship of logical to physical devices (see physical device).

memory — a term used to refer to any storage media for binary data.

modem — a device for processing computer data to a form that can be sent over a telephone line or radio link and which can receive such information and convert it again to computer data.

monitor — software or firmware that observes, supervises, controls, and verifies the operation of a system.

mother board — an electronic circuit board that supports one or more circuit boards, as the S-100 bus board in many CP/M systems.

multi-user operating system — an operating system that can be used by more than one user at a time.

null directory entry — a directory entry for a file that is empty (contains no information).

object file — the machine level program produced as the output of an assembly or compile operation.

octal — a number system in which each symbol represents a power of eight.

operating system — a group of programs that organizes a collection of hardware devices into an integrated working system that people can use.

output device — a peripheral used to display, store, or print information from a computer.

page — a 256 byte memory space in most microcomputer systems.

parallel interface — a peripheral connection in which information is sent to or from the computer one character at a time (contrast with serial interface).

parameters — information passed by the user to a program to control execution.

Pascal — a high level language named for Blaise Pascal. Pascal is highly user-oriented, easy to learn, and structured.

P-Code — the output coding of a Pascal compiler which must be interpreted at execution time.

peripheral — any part of the computer system external to the central processor to provide additional features as a printer, modem, or terminal.

physical device — a peripheral and its associated BIOS driver in CP/M. A *real* device as contrasted to the logical device seen by the program. CP/M manages the relationship of logical to physical devices.

PIP program — the CP/M peripheral interchange program used to load, print, punch, copy, or combine disk files.

pointer — a movable reference point in the editor normally located between the most recent character operated upon and the next character. At any given time it can be thought of as where the EDITOR is acting in your text.

preprocessor — a high-level language used to compile source code to a specific form that can be read by another compiler.

printer — a device that writes output data from a system to paper or other media. Popular types include the daisy wheel (using a circular daisy-like wheel for high quality printing) and the high-speed dot-matrix in which the characters are formed of closely spaced dots.

processor — the functional part of the computer system that reads and interprets instructions.

program — a series of instructions capable of producing a defined output from a given input.

program files — files used to store related instructions necessary to solve a particular problem (contrast with data files).

proprietary — refers to the exclusive right of a manufacturer to sell, copy, or use a program.

protected program — a program stored in computer memory that cannot be erased — as a program stored in ROM.

random files — files that are fixed in length and for which the time to access any record in the file is the same (contrast with sequential files).

record — a collection of related items treated as a unit. A unit of disk storage.

RESET operation — the clearing of computer registers and the initialization of the system. This is normally done automatically on power-on and from a pane switch thereafter.

ROM — read-only-memory. Computer storage in which data or programs are permanently or semi-permanently stored and which cannot be erased in normal circuit operation.

RS-232C — a standard type of serial interface used in computer systems.

S-100 bus — a standard type of computer bus used in many CP/M computer systems. Daughter boards are placed in 100-pin sockets on an S-100 mother board.

sector — a physical storage entity on a floppy disk.

sequential files — files in which the time to access any record in the file is a function of its distance from the beginning of the file (contrast with random files).

serial interface — a peripheral connection in which information is sent to or from the computer one bit at a time over a single circuit.

serial video terminal — a terminal connected to a computer with a serial interface, normally RS-232C.

single-step — the execution of a program one instruction at a time. This can be done using software (as with the CP/M DDT program) or with front panel hardware in certain computers.

software — computer resources with value because of their information content (contrast with hardware and firmware).

source program — a program in a language other than the machine language required by the computer and which must be converted before it can be executed.

spooler — a program that permits a user to continue with another program while printing.

structured programming — programming in an organized pattern such that the problem solution flow is easily followed.

system — a collection of men or machines organized to accomplish a specific function.

terminal—a device capable of sending and receiving information over a channel.

throughput output speed—the average speed of the computer in transmitting information to a peripheral.

transient program area (TPA)—that part of the computer memory that is not directly used by the CP/M, and which extends from 100H to the beginning of CP/M.

usable tracks—the physical units of storage on a disk that are accessible to the computer.

utility—a program that has a general purpose for a wide base of users.

video-mapped display—a video terminal in which the screen image is stored in the computer memory and constantly recreated from this memory. Altering this memory with the computer quickly alters the display. Useful for animation and games.

verify mode—a file transfer mode in PIP in which the resulting output file is compared with the original to insure its accuracy.

Index